SCANDALS

GRIPPING ACCOUNTS OF THE EXPOSED AND DEPOSED

SCANDALS

GRIPPING ACCOUNTS OF THE EXPOSED AND DEPOSED

SEAN CALLERY

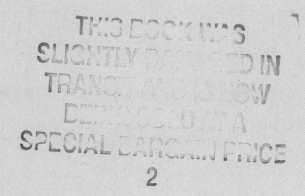

BCA

LONDON   NEW YORK   SYDNEY   TORONTO

A QUINTET BOOK

Copyright © 1992 Quintet Publishing Limited

This edition published 1992 by BCA
by arrangement with Quintet Publishing Limited

CN 6962

Reprinted 1993

This book was designed and produced by
Quintet Publishing Limited
6 Blundell Street
London N7 9BH

Project Editor: Laura Sandelson
Creative Director: Richard Dewing
Designer: Annie Moss
Editor: Rosemary Booton
Picture Researcher: Liz Eddison

Typeset in Great Britain by
Central Southern Typesetters, Eastbourne
Manufactured by
J Film Process Singapore Pte Ltd.
Printed in Singapore by
Star Standard Industries Private Ltd.

BRIGHT
BOOKS
15/12/00

CONTENTS

INTRODUCTION

Serge Stavisky

Guy Burgess

Ivan Boesky

What makes a scandal? Why should a blind eye be turned on one man's impropriety while another's is highlighted in the blazing spotlight of the public gaze? Can there be a link between the fraudsters, liars and pursuers of sex who create scandal? There can, in so far as the number of elements must combine to make a truly classifiable scandal.

First, there must be impropriety that offends the ethics of the society of the day. This could be sexual misconduct, fraud, or duplicity. Public outrage is an essential element in a scandal, so society's norms or acceptable behaviour must be wildly exceeded.

But this is not enough – after all, it happens every day around the globe. Scandals should ideally involve a public figure or organization: a politician like John Profumo or Edward Kennedy; a film star like Fatty Arbuckle; a member of the royal family like Edward VIII. Such luminaries can elevate the importance of an event even if they are only involved by chance. The presence of the Prince of Wales at a card table playing alongside a cheat, or the knowledge that Alger Hiss mixed with the likes of Roosevelt, Stalin and Churchill, is enough to push a misdeed towards the level of a scandal.

Sometimes simply being successful puts a person into this category – Serge Stavisky and Ivar Kreuger were no-bodies who became major figures, and then suffered for their fraud. An exception to this rule is spies, who by the nature of their work are rarely public figures. Here the act of betrayal is not enough to make a scandal, but ineptitude in exposing them (the Cambridge spies) or deceit in knowingly convicting them wrongly (Dreyfus and probably Alger Hiss) makes the scandal. Furthermore, if a major organization or institution is involved (such as the British government in the De Lorean scandal, or the American stock markets in the Boesky affair), the players are elevated to the level of public figures because of the prestige of their victim.

Finally, a true scandal is a revealed secret that someone has sought to cover up. This requirement can be ignored if the sheer scale of the misconduct is sufficiently massive. For example Byron rarely sought to conceal his wide-ranging sexual experiments. He was scandalous almost because of this, for the very relish with which he conducted

TED'S PAST: BRIBES, LIES & COWARDICE

FIGHT TO SAVE STAVISKY'S LIFE

NIXON ADMITS

Confessions of Christine

Richard Nixon

Robert Calvi

Donald Maclean

Fatty Arbuckle

his activities. Similarly, Ivan Boesky deceived his fellow-traders while carrying out his insider dealing, but "sang" when the authorities caught up with him. (A wag commented that "Ivan the Terrible" had been transformed into "Ivan the Tenor".)

One wonders how many careers could have been saved if the wrongdoer had blurted out the unhappy truth at the first opportunity. But human instinct leads man to try to conceal his mistakes, and very often the attempt to hide the truth achieves the same scandalous status as the misdeed itself. Some extra spice is added if there is an element of hypocrisy in the cover-up – television evangelist Jim Bakker's piety was shown to be less than skindeep, for example.

Thus a true scandal must involve what is considered improper behaviour with regard to sex, money, or power, by or linked to a public figure, which is then concealed. Why should a great scandal feature a public figure? Partly perhaps because obscure people do not attract attention, and can get away with worse behaviour. But most of us share a delight in seeing a big shot get his come-uppance, or a respected figure exposed as a hypocrite. This is linked to our jealousy at the importance such people have attained, and how it has been abused.

This leads us to consider if there are certain types of people who attract scandal, and the answer is surely "yes". Most of the stories in this book feature as a protagonist someone who was ambitious and dissatisfied with their lot. Fatty Arbuckle wanted to show his power by conquering another starlet; Roberto Calvi sought money, prestige and power; and the Cambridge spies thought they were furthering world peace (though they probably relished the many ironies of their double lives).

Doubtless there have been worse indiscretions, corruption and affairs which were successfully hushed up, leaving a relieved celebrity to do wrong another day. It's all part of the fun of life.

Byron

THE WHOREMONGER POET

Lord Byron was a leader of the Romantic school of poetry. He was also "mad, bad and dangerous to know" according to one of his countless lovers. His antics shocked even the tolerant Regency society which adored him.

ABOVE

Lady Caroline Lamb, one of the most celebrated of Byron's numerous lovers, famously dubbed him as "mad, bad and dangerous to know".

During the travels which inspired his first success, Byron spent a fortune on prostitutes and enjoyed many affairs. He once accidentally intercepted a cart carrying one of his past conquests wriggling in a sack. She was to be dumped in the sea after her husband discovered her infidelity, until Byron spirited her away.

Rumours of such exploits burnished his reputation in London, and made him especially attractive to wilful young women in high society. One such was Lady Caroline Lamb, wife of Lord Melbourne, who wrote the famous description of him as "mad, bad and dangerous to know" while describing their affair in her diary. Ending the relationship, Byron commenced an affair with his half-sister Augusta Leigh, which resulted in the birth of a daughter. In addition to boasting of his incest to the gossips of London, he used it as a theme in his novel in verse, "The Bride of Abydos", which was a bestseller of its day.

Perhaps to reduce his notoriety, Byron married Anne Isabella Mil-

"I awoke one morning and found myself famous," wrote Lord Byron of the immediate success of the first parts of his poem "Childe Harold's Pilgrimage" in 1812. It describes his tours of Portugal, Spain and the Balkans in a style typical of the Romantic poets, who were convinced of their own heightened sensibilities and relishing a gloomy, doomed perspective. However, his real life was less romantic than deeply sordid and amoral – so much so that after his death his friends burned his memoirs rather than reveal his love of whores, boys, and his incest.

George Gordon Byron was born in 1788, and inherited the title of baron at the age of ten. He had an unhappy childhood, taunted by his school-friends because of his heavy limp, caused by a deformed right foot. He was also prone to obesity. When he went up to Cambridge in 1805 he was renowned as a particularly enthusiastic (and sometimes aggressive) customer of whores. There he also developed his sexual interest in young boys, and took a mistress whom he sometimes dressed in boys' clothes and passed off as male.

BELOW

Byron's half-sister August Leigh, with whom he had an affair, resulting in the birth of a daughter.

Lady Byron, formerly
Anne Isabella Milbanke,
was naive in the ways of
love, but brilliant in the
practice of mathematics.

banke, an innocent and highly intelligent woman, in 1815. He persisted in a libidinous and extravagant lifestyle (bailiffs' visits were almost as common as those of his mistresses) and when his wife was recovering from the birth of their child she returned to her parents. They were horrified to discover that Byron had frequently sodomized her, and she never went back to him.

Byron was prone to bouts of gloominess and self-pity. Soon such indulgence could be fully justified as the stories of his indecencies, incest and drunkenness transformed him from the darling of London society to a figure of hate. The invitations dwindled and were replaced by snubs. He fled England in April 1816 having made a girl called Clair Clarimont pregnant (another daughter, Allegra, who died very young). Byron then passed the time in Geneva with another romantic poet, Percy Bysshe Shelley.

The roaming poet moved on to Italy, seducing the woman of the house in the lodgings he took, and commencing numerous other affairs. The sale of his estate enabled him to live in some style, and his home became virtually a brothel. He was also as indiscreet in his dabbling in revolutionary politics as he was in his sexual activities. Byron's antics shocked even the cosmopolitan Venetians.

He set off for Greece, abandoning yet another mistress, Teresa, wife of Count Alessandro Guiccioli. Here he began training troops to fight for independence from the Turks, but succumbed to fever and died at the age of 37. Lady Caroline Lamb chanced across his funeral procession, and as a result succumbed to mental illness which lasted the rest of her life.

Byron has been called "the patron saint of romantic liberalism" and is remembered for his flowing verse which satirized hypocrisy and social convention. Byronic heroes are aloof, cynical, rebellious and melancholy.

AN UNLIKELY DAUGHTER

Byron's wife Anne was a mathematician, and their daughter Ada Augusta followed her mother to become the world's first computer programmer, working on Charles Babbage's mechanical calculating machines. The high-level computer language of 1983, ADA, was named after her. The contrast with her scandal-laden father could hardly be greater.

Byron was all of these things, but he was also a focus of scandal because of his extravagant sexual licence. He would surely have been a notorious figure in whatever time he lived.

The Card Cheat & The Prince Of Wales

When Sir William Gordon-Cumming was accused of cheating at cards while playing with the Prince of Wales, his smart set friends deserted him. The story became late Victorian England's biggest society scandal.

The Prince of Wales (later Edward VII) was a dandy, womanizer and gambler – and he set the tone for the rest of high society in the 1880s and 90s. A visit from him brought prestige and the smart set in his tow, and he had to be royally entertained with feasting and gambling if his host wished to remain a valued friend.

Thus it was that on the night of Monday 8 September 1890, a party gathered at Tranby Croft in Yorkshire, England, home of Sir Arthur Wilson. He was a rich shipbuilder with a socially ambitious wife, and their guests had come up for the race meeting at Doncaster. Among the guests were the Earl and Countess of Coventry, General Owen Williams (a former equerry of the Prince who shared his love of racing) and Sir Willian Alexander Gordon-Cumming, Bt, a lieutenant-colonel in the Scots Guards with a private income of £80,000 ($388,800) a year – a fortune at the time. Gordon-Cumming was something of a snob and was not particularly popular, but he had helped the Prince's sexual exploits by putting his town house at "Bertie's" disposal.

A game of baccarat was proposed. Although playing this casino-like gambling game was illegal, it was a favourite with the Prince, who travelled with his own cards and counters. A dozen of the party settled down at 10.30pm to play baccarat banque, with

THE WASTREL PRINCE

Bertie, Prince of Wales, virtually bankrupted a number of his hosts because of his high expectations of the entertainments they should provide. He expected his friends to keep up with all his enthusiasms, and at least one, Christopher Sykes, was financially ruined by trying to do just that. His mother, Queen Victoria, mistrusted his feckless ways, seeing in them many of the antics of her ancestors and little of her upright and respectable husband.

The Prince had numerous mistresses, including the actresses Lillie Langtry and Sarah Bernhardt, French showgirl La Gouloue, Harriet Mordaunt, Lady Daisy Brooke, and, last of all, Alice Keppel. He usually chose to have affairs with married women so that any pregnancy could be assumed to be by her husband.

Along with his love of women, he enjoyed hunting, shooting, racing, eating and drinking, watching light comedies, and gambling. A charming and charismatic figure, Bertie was a weak character who saw no reason not to exploit the many advantages his birth had brought him. He reached the throne at last in 1901 at the age of 59, and although he dutifully undertook his duties, he continued to mix with the smart set, and switched the centre of royal life from Windsor to Buckingham Palace in London.

ABOVE

While accusations of cheating were being made behind closed doors, the house party at Tranby Croft was photographed on 11 September 1890. Sir Gordon-Cumming is in the centre of the front row, next to the seated Prince of Wales.

the Prince acting as banker and the other guests split into two groups. The aim of this game is to bet on whether you can score nine on the face value of your cards. If a player goes "bust", he sits out and another in the group takes the next hand.

During the evening, several in the group noticed that Gordon-Cumming was cheating by adding to his stake if he saw it had won, and removing a counter or two if the stake was lost. He thus increased his winnings and minimized his losses. They watched him more closely when the game was played again the next evening, and became certain the rich army officer was cheating. His winnings for the two days amounted to £228 ($1,110). After the day's racing on 10 September, six of the male guests conferred about what to do with the blackguard in their midst. They decided the Prince must be told, and that Gordon-Cumming must sign a declaration swearing never to play cards again.

The officer denied the charge vehemently, but eventually agreed to sign the paper to avoid gossip about the incident. The other players also signed the incriminating document. Gordon-Cumming was naive if he thought this would end the matter. Gossip was the lifeblood of the smart set, and the Prince of Wales' current mistress, Lady Daisy Brooke, was known as the "Babbling Brooke" because of her inability to keep a secret. Was there any doubt that Bertie would confide in her about the unpleasantness during their intimate pillow talk?

Needless to say the story of the officer caught cheating at cards with the Prince of Wales spread rapidly through high society, becoming common knowledge in London and Paris. Gordon-Cumming decided to salvage his damaged reputation by bringing a civil action for slander against his original accusers. This would mean bringing the whole story into the open and calling those involved – including the

Prince – as witnesses. Edward was appalled, for he had bad memories of the last time he has been called as a court witness, at the divorce case of Sir Charles and Lady Harriet Mordaunt, when the Prince had been named as one of her lovers.

The trial took up nine days of June 1891, in the middle of a heat wave. Gordon-Cumming's lawyer Sir Edward Clarke (later to act for Oscar Wilde in an equally sensational trial) questioned the reliability of the evidence of cheating, and suggested that his client was being sacrificed to avoid a public scandal for the Prince of Wales. The defendants were revealed to be a foppish and decadent band who followed a life of fashion, fun and gambling. Such company did not reflect well on the future king, who was himself booed and hissed when he appeared at the opening day of Ascot races while the jury considered its verdict. The public's disapproval had been increased by reports of his unimpressive, nervous display in court.

The jury found against Gordon-Cumming, a decision which surprised those who had watched the trial. Press coverage focused on the revelations of the lifestyle of the Prince, who was condemned as a "wastrel and whoremonger". There were those who suggested that the king-to-be, and not the officer, should have signed a pledge against cards.

Gordon-Cumming's fiancée, a rich American called Florence Garner, had stood by him all along and he married her on the day after the trial. But her husband became a social pariah, was dismissed from the army and expelled from his clubs. He remained bitter about the friends who had deserted him until his death in 1938.

The Dreyfus Affair

Picture the scene: a man languishes in a primitive hut on Devil's Island off the coast of French Guyana. He is shackled, watched night and day, allowed little exercise, and offered minimal treatment for the fevers from which he suffers. What terrible deeds did he commit to merit this punishment? The answer is none. The innocent man was Alfred Dreyfus, and his case had spurred France into a frenzy of anti-Semitism and false "honour".

Dreyfus was born into a wealthy Jewish family in Alsace on 19 October 1859. He decided not to follow his father into textile manufacturing, and resolved on a military career, which began in 1882. Well-educated (he spoke German and Italian), a little arrogant with a haughty manner, Dreyfus rose to the rank of captain in seven years. He married and started a family.

On 15 October 1894, his world fell apart. While assigned to the War Ministry, he was accused of selling secrets to the German military attaché. Dreyfus protested his innocence, but handwriting experts claimed a note offering the information was written by him. It had been retrieved from a waste-paper basket in the German embassy by the cleaner, a French agent who handed it over.

Dreyfus was convicted on 22 December, stripped of his military honours early in January, and soon began his life sentence on Devil's Island. He left behind a nation whose anti-Semitic instincts had been stirred by the treason, and whose people had filled the streets shouting "Death to the Jew".

The next year, 1896, a new Chief of Intelligence, Lieutenant-Colonel Georges Picquart, discovered that the note had been written by an officer still serving in the army, Major Esterhazy.

The Dreyfus Affair divided the French nation over a number of years. A Jewish officer convicted on false spying allegations was kept in imprisonment for years while the Army concealed his innocence behind a patriotic front.

LE TRAITRE
Dégradation d'Alfred Dreyfus

A NATION DIVIDED

The Dreyfus Affair ran for 12 years but its peak came in 1898-9 when France was the scene of violent street clashes and a virulent press campaign. In a way the Jewish captain was irrelevant to these scenes, which indicated a nation divided by philosophy, laced with anti-Semitism. On the one hand the "Dreyfusards" (intellectuals, socialists and radical groups) championed the freedom of the individual. They accused their opponents (the Army and the Church) of undermining the Republic and hoping to set up an authoritarian regime. The end of the Dreyfus Affair did not end the factionalism, which lasted throughout the Third Republic until 1940.

ABOVE

A cartoon showing the public disgrace inflicted on Dreyfus by his fellow officer, at a time when honour was held in the highest esteem.

RIGHT

There is a French saying: "Truth lies at the bottom of the well". This Dreyfusard board game takes the metaphor literally and asks players to journey towards the truth.

THE REAL VILLAIN

Major Marie Charles Ferdinand Walsin Esterhazy was a womanizer and gambler who was constantly in need of money. He entered the German embassy on 20 July 1894 and offered an astounded military attaché, Colonel von Schwarzkoppen, information about the French Army, its manoeuvres, equipment and intelligence reports. Although the Germans were slow to respond, Esterhazy began sending documents in September. The major was a fine orator, and at the subsequent trials, he movingly evoked the sense of honour which binds men of war together, inspiring bursts of applause from his fellow officers. He later took up a partnership in a brothel to which he supplied the names of 1,500 potential clients, many of them being these colleagues. When his luck ran out, he slipped away, and lived quietly in England using the name Comte de Violemont. He died in 1923.

This information proved very inconvenient for his superiors, who considered the whole miserable affair to be over and had no wish to admit that a dreadful mistake had been made at a court martial.

Esterhazy was an unscrupulous character who proceeded to invent new evidence against the convict, aided by a Major Henry, who forged documents naming Dreyfus as a spy and suppressed others which showed the reverse. Both made much of the code of honour in the French Army under which it was the most terrible imposition to even imply that one of their number had acted wrongly. There was talk of a "patriotic forgery". Esterhazy stood trial but was greatly helped by sympathetic judges and a crowd which heckled anyone who supported Dreyfus. The judges deliberated for three minutes before acquitting him. Picquart, who had at one stage been posted to North Africa to keep him out of the way, was later arrested himself. The military was closing ranks.

Meanwhile, however, some sections of society had picked up on rumours about the case, and slowly a band of "Dreyfusards" was formed. This included the famous novelist Emile Zola, who on 13 January 1898 published an open letter in the newspaper *Aurore* under the headline "J'accuse". It was a remarkable piece, naming those who had helped to convict an innocent man while acquitting the guilty party. The paper sold 200,000 copies in a day, and the contents of its front page divided France into two camps: those who believed a foreign conspiracy against the nation had been stopped, and those who felt that the rights of an individual to a fair trial were sacrosanct. Zola was tried for libel and given the maximum one-year sentence, being found not guilty at his appeal.

This tiny compound was Dreyfus' jail, on a small island off the South American coast.

French writer Emile Zola was a leading figure in the fight to free Dreyfus, and his impassioned plea for justice was a key point in the saga.

Later that year, Major Henry killed himself by slitting his own throat after confessing his part in falsifying and withholding documents. Esterhazy fled to Belgium and then to England.

Dreyfus had been unaware of many of these events from his lonely prison, but continued public pressure led to his return for a retrial in 1899. It was a pathetically haggard and prematurely aged figure who came back to his homeland and embraced his wife for the first time in five years.

Surprisingly the judge upheld the original verdict. When the President of the Republic pardoned him, the Dreyfus family were relieved, but not satisfied. A long campaign finally earned a retrial and in July 1906 the civilian court of appeals reversed all his convictions. Dreyfus was reinstated in the army, and awarded the Légion d'Honneur. He served his country in World War One and died on 12 July 1935.

THE MARCONI SHARE DEALERS

Britain's Liberal government of 1912 came near to collapse when it emerged that three of its ministers had purchased shares in a company about to receive a government contract.

Herbert Asquith, the prime minister who supported Lloyd George during the scandal, is welcomed home from a 1925 trip by his wife and the Welsh politician.

The Marconi Affair was typical of political scandals in that what actually happened was of less importance than the manner in which the facts emerged. The story begins in 1910 when the radio giant the Marconi Company approached the British government suggesting that it set up a network of radio stations to allow instant communication between the various parts of the British Empire. Radio was in its infancy, but its potential value was becoming apparent. For example this was the year when the Canada-bound murderer Dr Crippen

was "captured" by a radio message from the captain of his ship alerting police to his presence.

The idea was approved by the end of 1911, but no announcement was to be made until the contract was finalized. On 9 April 1912, the managing director of the Marconi Company, Godfrey Isaacs, dined at the Savoy hotel in London with his brothers Harry and Rufus. Rufus was Attorney General in Asquith's Liberal government. Godfrey told his siblings of an excellent opportunity: the American Marconi Company was planning to issue 1.4 million dollar shares, and if they bought now at the pre-market price, they would make a killing.

Harry snatched up 50,000 shares, selling 10,000 to Rufus a week later. The Attorney General enthused to his friends and fellow ministers David Lloyd George (Chancellor of the Exchequer) and Alexander Murray and both purchased 1,000 shares from him at £2 ($10). The next day Murray secretly bought a further 2,500 shares with Liberal Party funds. When the shares came onto the market, they peaked at £4 ($20) before dropping back to half that figure. The three ministers made various buys and sells, ironically resulting in an overall loss of £1,700 ($8,228) for Isaacs and a £213 ($1,000) loss for the others. Their behaviour can best be described as foolish.

Over the summer, the government unsuccessfully attempted to force through the Marconi contract during the parliamentary recess, while rumours began to circulate in the City about government members buying and selling shares using information not publicly available. The story refused to die, and by October the government had been forced into appointing a select committee to investigate both the Marconi contract and the share-dealing allegations. On 11 October Rufus Isaacs told an excited House of Commons that neither he nor government members had had "one single transaction with the shares of that company". He chose not to point out that they had, however, bought shares in its American sister. This economy with the truth was ill-advised, as the slow-moving committee crept towards discovering the deals itself.

A report on its investigation in the French newspaper *Le Matin* gave Isaacs the chance to put the record straight, rather than have the facts pulled like teeth from him by the committee. He sued for libel, and at the court hearing his lawyer went to considerable trouble to make a statement admitting that

ministers had bought some shares in the American Marconi Company. He even attempted to prove that there had been no dishonesty by commenting that the unhappy politicians had failed to make a profit anyway.

This attempt to kill off the story failed when Sir Rufus appeared before the committee on 25 March, and was forced to concede that three ministers had bought shares, unavailable to the public, on favourable terms, and had sold them when the price rose and bought more when the price fell.

A previously compliant British press took up the story with a vengeance. When Lloyd George gave evidence three days later, his performance was risible. The reforming Chancellor, pioneer of old age pensions in 1909 and unemployment insurance in 1911, was now presenting himself as a poor man trying to build a little nest egg. Reputations were further damaged with the revelation that a government officer was involved with secret share dealings. The facts had thus been served up in the worst way: piece by piece over a number of months, generously garnished with rumours of impropriety, and with Isaacs' speech to the House of Commons revealed to be an attempt at a cover-up.

Alexander Murray had already left the country, and Rufus Isaacs and Lloyd George offered to resign, but Prime Minister Asquith decided not to accept their resignations. He knew that the select committee had a government majority, and would prepare a whitewash report. It duly did, but some members were so appalled at its evasions that they released their own "minority" report, which was less equivocal. At a heated Commons debate in June, a motion was passed accepting that the ministers concerned regretted their actions, and the Marconi Affair was over. Asquith abandoned his thoughts of any early election, but was grateful not to have lost one of his most able ministers in Lloyd George, and possibly even more.

KNIGHTHOOD, ANYONE?

This was not the only financial scandal with which Lloyd George was identified. After becoming Prime Minister, his administration handled the already corrupt honours system with unheard of indiscretion. A place in the honours lists could now be openly purchased with a donation to Liberal Party funds. For £10,000 ($48,600) you could have a knighthood, a baronetcy would cost three times that figure, and peerages started at £50,000 ($243,000). Brokers touted for business with letters selling honours. One stressed that there were "only five knighthoods left for the June list . . . [and] it is not likely that the next Government will give so many honours, and this is really an excellent opportunity". From 1917 onwards, Lloyd George created baronetcies at double the previous rate, and created the OBE of which 25,000 were awarded in four years. The reward was at least £1 million ($5 million) given to Liberal Party funds.

Fatty Arbuckle's Fall

LEFT

A baby-like face above a huge body, Fatty Arbuckle exploited his comic figure to become a major film star.

Wild parties, sex and murder were the ingredients of a Hollywood scandal that ended the career of comic Fatty Arbuckle.

NEW SENSATION IN ARBUCKLE CASE!

In September 1921 Fatty Arbuckle was a Hollywood star with a big future. The antics of the baby-faced, 21-stone (133kg) comic actor were popular with audiences, and prized by top producer Mack Sennett. He had just agreed a $3 million contract with Paramount. Within days he was reviled as an alleged rapist and murderer, and cinemas resounded with booing at his films. Although never convicted, Fatty Arbuckle's career (and virtually his life) was ended by a classic Hollywood sex scandal.

When he was born in Kansas in 1887, Roscoe Arbuckle already weighed 16lb (7kg). He made his stage debut at the age of eight, but worked as a plumber's mate and a farm labourer before landing an $18-a-week singing job when he was 15. His father gave

him little encouragement, blaming Roscoe's size as a baby for the death of his wife; but it was Arbuckle's physical attributes – a huge body topped by an expressive baby face – that got him into movies.

Bizarrely, his major break came after a picnic by the Rio Grande. He exchanged insults with the Mexican revolutionary Pancho Villa, and flung an apple pie which was promptly returned. Thus was born the idea of the manic pie-fight, which he took onto the screen and which gave his career a massive boost. Audiences began to love his angelic face and his surprising agility as he lampooned around on the silver screen.

By 1917, he was writing and directing a string of comedies, having moved to Jesse Lasky's Artcraft with Mack

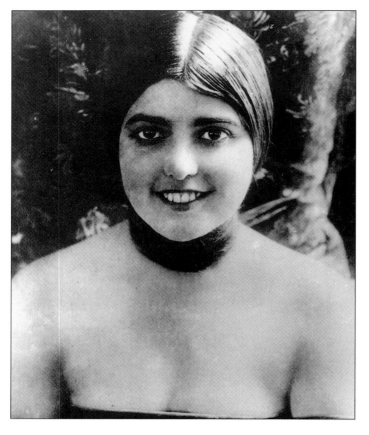

The last photograph ever taken of starlet Virginia Rappe shows an attractive woman with deep, dark eyes. Fatty Arbuckle was captivated by her, but she did not seem to return any of his affection.

had given half of Mack Sennett's Keystone company a dose of venereal disease did not lessen his desire, which was stimulated by the power his new contract brought.

By Monday the party was still swinging, and Arbuckle was ambling about in pyjamas, carpet slippers and a bathrobe when he came across Rappe who was heading for the bathroom. He grabbed her and took her into room 1219. A short time later loud screams silenced the party and some of the guests clustered anxiously outside Arbuckle's bedroom, where the screams were coming from. Shouts for the door to be opened were met with more screams. The hotel's assistant manager was summoned to unlock the door, upon which Arbuckle danced out, with Rappe's hat perched daintily above his cherubic face. Behind him, Rappe was prone on the bed, her clothes ripped off her, groaning. "I'm dying. I'm dying. He hurt me", she reportedly moaned.

Three days later she was dead from a ruptured bladder. This could have been caused by the champagne bottle Arbuckle allegedly assaulted her with, or simply from the impact of his huge body being forced on top of her.

Newspaper headlines about the orgy that ended in death wrecked Arbuckle's career even before the inquest found him "criminally responsible" and he was charged with murder. Suddenly benign, jovial Fatty Arbuckle cavorting around on the screen wasn't funny anymore.

Powerful people were keen to see Arbuckle convicted at his November trial. Some studio bosses disliked his refusal to kowtow to them, and the San Francisco District Attorney was after the Californian governorship and needed to win a newsworthy case. The trial judge saw moral implications in the case, saying, "We are trying ourselves . . . our present-day social conditions, our present-day looseness of thought and lack of social balance".

The trial evidence shocked the pub-

Sennett. In that year he narrowly avoided a major scandal after an all-night party in Boston. An inquisitive Bostonian called the police after he spotted Arbuckle taking off his clothes on a table along with several girls. It emerged that a dozen girls had been paid $1,000 to attend the party. Apparently it took ten times that figure in bribes to local officials to forget about the incident.

Four years later Paramount signed him up for $3 million. Ever the keen party-thrower, Fatty Arbuckle decided to organize a truly wild celebration at the St Francis Hotel in San Francisco, beginning on Saturday 3 September 1921. Among the 50 or so guests invited to the twelfth-floor suite was a minor starlet, Virginia Rappe, whose presence Arbuckle had specifically requested. She was a 25-year-old model from Chicago with a fresh, innocent face that had landed her a number of small-time roles. Arbuckle had been vying for her attention for five years, but she found him unattractive. Tales that she

The Fatty Arbuckle Scandal and its surrounding publicity led Hollywood studio heads to fear censorship and a big clean-up operation if they did not improve the image of Hollywood. The result was the Motional Picture Producers and Distributors of America, a self-regulatory body headed by US Postmaster-General Will H Hays. The Hays office successfully fought off pressure groups and smoothed over stories of Hollywood vice, while encouraging the following of an unenforcable purity code in pictures. It also supported producers who ensured that vile on-screen behaviour always got its just desserts.

lic. Arbuckle had winked at friends as he snatched the starlet, saying "This is what I've been waiting for". He was alleged to have penetrated her with a lump of ice after starting off with the champagne bottle. When the door had been unlocked his initial amiability had quickly turned to a fit of temper and he had yelled "Shut up, or I'll throw you out of the window". His lawyers countered by suggesting that Rappe had slept with half of Hollywood and had had five abortions. These could have caused the scars on her

bladder which the prosecution claimed were the result of Arbuckle landing on top of her. All these claims only added to the excited newspaper coverage of the trial.

Public adulation for Arbuckle turned to hate. Cowboys shot a cinema screen showing one of his films in Wyoming, and women tore down the screen in Hartford, Connecticut. Arbuckle's reputation would hardly have survived one trial, let alone the three it took before a set of jurors finally pronounced him innocent of murder on 12 April 1922. The verdict hardly mattered; by then, Arbuckle's Paramount contract had been cancelled, together with showings of all his films. Producer Adolph Zukor made him the first Hollywood star to be put on a blacklist. The man who had been considered funnier than Charlie Chaplin (indeed, had lent him the trousers which became part of the famous tramp costume) could only direct a few comedies under the pseudonym William Goodrich.

Fatty Arbuckle died of a heart attack on 28 June 1933 aged 46. Ironically, he had just returned from a party to celebrate signing a contract with Warner Brothers that could have begun his comeback. Browsing through the titles of the many films he made, the story of his downfall was told in advance: *Fatty's Magic Party; A Flirt's Mistake; The Village Scandal; He Did and He Didn't*, and *Fickle Fatty's Fall*.

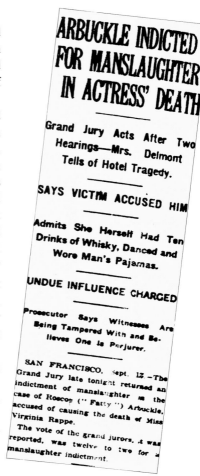

BELOW

Arbuckle and his attorneys plan their campaign against the first-degree murder charge.

The Fraudulent Match King

Ivar Kreuger was an international figure, a maker of loans to governments, a millionaire entrepreneur. But his financial empire was a sham, and when it fell, skeletons rattled in cupboards around the globe.

Ivar Kreuger was born on 2 March 1880 in the Swedish seaside town of Kalmar. His father helped to run a shipping business and was the local Russian consul. Kreuger trained as an engineer in Stockholm and at the age of 20 left his homeland to pursue his fortune in America.

Ever the opportunist, Kreuger exploited a chance that came his way when he found almost-completed plans for a small house left by a previous lodger in his Chicago rooms. He waited for the client to call, explained that the architect had been called away but that as a fellow-professional he would finish the job. His draughtsman's skills did the rest, and he made $50. The story illustrates Kreuger's ability to make the most of an opportunity, and the love for a gamble which was central to his character.

The ambitious Swede went on to earn a reasonable living over the next eight years through a number of projects. He built bridges in Mexico, worked for a New York construction company, and supervised steelwork installations in Johannesburg where he also ran a restaurant for a while. Recognizing the potential of the newly invented reinforced concrete, he built an office block in the centre of Stockholm in record time. From 1908 to 1913 the construction firm he had set up with his partner, Paul Toll, flourished.

Kreuger wanted more of a challenge than running Kreuger and Toll, as it did not satisfy his gambler's urge. In 1913 he branched out into the safety match business which Scandinavia's abundant forests supplied. This was a highly competitive industry with too many suppliers chasing too little business. The charismatic entrepreneur took it by storm, uniting ten small factories into one company, and later swallowing up his largest rival, Jonkoping-Vulcan, to form Swedish Match. But he wanted more.

Many countries refused to import various goods, including matches, and insisted on all supplies being sourced domestically. Kreuger began to buy up match factories throughout Europe, often using the tactic of sending out scouts to locate struggling concerns and make a derisory offer. Kreuger would then arrive like the cavalry to "rescue" the hapless company. Shrewd investment and ruthless acquisition of rivals would follow, and the Kreuger match empire grew.

As governments struggled to cope with the disastrous financial consequences of World War One, Kreuger the deal-maker would turn up with a generous loan to be made over the next few years and repaid on favourable terms – in return for the match-making monopoly. He found a ready welcome: Poland, Greece, Yugoslavia, Hungary, Romania, Turkey, Peru, Ecuador and Guatemala all signed on the dotted line.

So far the only scent of scandal was in Kreuger's forceful negotiating tactics with governments who were desperate for his cash. Now he decided to raid the biggest source of cash, America, for some audacious deals. From 1922 onwards, Kreuger built a labyrinth of interlinked companies across Europe which eventually comprised more than 400 subsidiaries. Key firms were staffed by "yes men" who would sign the accounts Kreuger prepared which grossly exaggerated their assets. Sometimes the books would be cooked with references to non-existent property deals, or imaginary licences. American investors eager to make money away from their own country's tax requirements happily put money into Kreuger's impressive empire. They were reassured to receive regular dividends. What they did not realize was that they were being paid with their own money, which was shuffled around between subsidiaries. In the meantime, Kreuger was transferring the bulk of their capital to his own accounts in Switzerland and Liechtenstein.

By 1927 Kreuger was able to provide the French government with a loan of £15 million ($75 million) at only 5 per cent interest. The French were so grateful they awarded him with the Grand Cross of the Legion of Honour, in addition, of course, to the match monopoly. It was a triumph for Kreuger, but it stretched his finances to the limit.

THE SCHOOL CHEAT

Kreuger had a reputation as a swindler at school. He ran a scheme in which each boy in a group would concentrate on his best subject, then share his work with his associates in return for their efforts in other subjects. He stole exam papers and managed to sell them, and even sold advance information on the results.

Kreuger must have realized this, but he was riding such a wave of success and popularity that he was soon tempted into his major mistake. He loaned 500 million marks ($125 million) to Germany on very generous terms in return for the marketing monopoly on matches. He was already the only producer of matches in the country, but cheap Russian imports were damaging the trade.

The timing was poor. American shares fell through the floor in the Wall Street Crash of 1929 and this led to a world cash crisis in 1930. The loan repayments slowed to a trickle, and Kreuger was suddenly short of money. He began to move large amounts of money between banks, using the receipt for each transaction as a guarantee on borrowed cash. When this and other swindles were not enough, he used the letterhead on a letter to him from Mussolini to forge 42 Italian Treasury bills for £500,000 ($2.5 million) to bolster his companies' audited accounts.

The forgery was discovered when Kreuger – still the toast of the financial markets – attempted a deal with American International Telephone and Telegraph in 1932. They wanted to see the books of a Kreuger company, and he knew these showed a shortfall of $7 million.

At last the empire began to crumble, and Kreuger could see on the faces of his business associates that they knew he had perpetrated a gigantic fraud. On the night of 11 March 1932, Ivar Kreuger shot himself through the heart in his apartment in the Avenue Victor Emmanuel in Paris.

Unravelling the web of his complex businesses took some time and it was several months before the financial world realized that it had been taken for a ride which had cost it a fortune. Of $148.5 million paid over by American investors, $144 million had disappeared into Kreuger's own accounts in Switzerland and Liechtenstein.

Worried crowds gather opposite the New York Stock Exchange during the Wall Street Crash of 1929 that triggered Kreuger's fall.

YOUR COUNTRY OR YOUR LOVER?

RIGHT

The Prince of Wales and Wallis Simpson at Biarritz in 1934, the year their affair began.

Edward VIII gave up his throne for the woman he loved, a twice-divorced American called Wallis Simpson. Their affair caused a sensation and a national crisis. Yet with their fascist leanings, they might have returned to Britain as Hitler's servants.

Edward, Prince of Wales, led a life many dreamed of while he waited to inherit the throne. He travelled the world, met important people, was guest of honour at the very best parties, and had a string of mistresses. Yet that series of relationships was based not on a desire for companionship or sex, but on a tremendous emotional vulnerability. The weak and fun-loving Edward felt stifled amid the pompous protocol of royal life, and loved escaping to his own more relaxed set.

Edward first got to know Wallis Simpson during a weekend at his Fort Belvedere residence in Windsor, England at the end of January, 1932. She was a flirty socialite, and best friend to his long-standing mistress, fellow-American Thelma Furness. Mrs Simpson was a determined social climber, and her clever and witty conversation gained her acceptance in the

BELOW

Lady Thelma Furness, twin sister of Gloria Vanderbilt, and lover of the Prince of Wales until Wallis Simpson took her place while she was abroad.

HITLER'S KING?

Was Edward VIII prepared to take up the throne again if Hitler invaded Britain? The answer could be yes, for both Edward and Wallis were sympathetic to the fascist policies adopted by Hitler and Mussolini.
● In June 1935 the Prince said in a speech that the British should "stretch forth the hand of friendship to the Germans".
● The British secret service was worried by Wallis' fascist contacts.
● Edward was very close to the German ambassador and expressed his annoyance at the British government's animosity towards Hitler.
● On 20 April 1936 the King sent Hitler a birthday telegram.
● Sensitive information given to the King found its way to Berlin.
● In August 1936 the King went on a Mediterranean cruise to visit countries with right-wing governments, to the dismay of Britain's rulers.
● During the couple's Venice honeymoon, the Duke gave crowds the fascist salute.
● In 1937 the Windsors toured Nazi Germany and met Hitler.
● During World War Two, there was contact between Germany and the Duke which suggests that the idea of him returning to a Nazi Britain as King was mooted. However, nothing was definitely agreed.

highest circles, together with toleration for her more reserved husband Ernest.

Thelma Furness went on an extended holiday two years later, and at her request the now well-established Wallis Simpson looked after the Prince. When Thelma returned, she had been replaced as his mistress.

The affair blossomed, and Wallis accompanied Edward to many of his engagements, usually with Ernest chugging along behind for the sake of

A nervous Duke of Windsor prepares to address the nation in his famous abdication speech.

The Duke of Windsor and his bride in France on 4 June 1937, the day after their wedding.

with which he handled state affairs soon weakened. It was so clear that he had no interest in the documents sent to him, and that all the royal decisions were actually made by Wallis Simpson, that officials began withholding sensitive information from the monarch. Meanwhile, Wallis ensured that palace life ran along the informal, sociable lines that Edward enjoyed, vetting guest lists and menus, and bringing their café society friends onto the royal circuit, much to the annoyance of the rest of the royal family, particularly Edward's mother Queen Mary.

This annoyance turned to alarm when the Simpsons divorced on 27 October, enabling her to marry the king the following summer. Prime Minister Baldwin expressed his concern to Edward, who replied that he would marry Wallis Simpson even if he had to renounce the throne. He told the rest of his family this news over the

appearances. Within a year the relationship was common knowledge in society circles, although the British press declined to reveal it to the general public. The arrangement was tolerated so long as Edward was a carefree prince: it would be different when he became king.

His father George V died on 20 January 1936. The emotionally insecure prince grieved deeply, both for the King, and for the way of life he would now lose. He moved into Buckingham Palace reluctantly, and the initial vigour

THE KING'S MISTRESS

Wallis Simpson was born on 19 June 1895 into a well-off Southern family. Marrying pioneer aviator Earl Winfield Spencer when she was 20, she discovered him to be a jealous and cruel alcoholic, and despite an attempt at reconciliation, they divorced in 1927. By now she had had a number of affairs and a difficult abortion in 1925 had ended her chances of having children. She had also met Ernest Simpson, a successful businessman, and they married in England in 1928. A dignified, quiet man, he tolerated her relationship with Edward for many years.

Though no great beauty, Wallis could be amusing and high-spirited, and high society took to her. Almost from the start of their affair she exerted a powerful influence over Edward, but, ironically, she claimed that she would rather have been mistress of the King than wife of a royal in exile.

next few days, but then began to suggest that a morganatic marriage might be possible. This would have allowed him to remain as king but his wife would not become queen, and nor would any children inherit the crown. Baldwin advised him that his suggestion required a special Bill to be passed in Parliament, and that this would be unlikely to succeed. This was based on the view that the British public – still in the dark about the affair – would not accept Wallis in the role of the King's wife. Her nationality did not help, but the chief problem was her image as a flighty socialite and divorcée.

The story finally broke on 2 December, after the Bishop of Bradford made a speech to a Diocesan conference in which he implied that the King was lacking in the moral and spiritual dedication required for his role. "We hope that he is aware of this need", he said. "Some of us wish that he gave more positive signs of such awareness." The comments of an obscure bishop gave the British press their chance to break silence, and they seized it with a vengeance. The general public were told the tale of the affair, and they did not like what they read, demonstrating in London with signs calling "Wally" a "whore", and pleading "Save our Edward VIII". Ironically, the King who was about to sacrifice his crown for his heart was very popular with his people, because he had visited them extensively in earlier years and had the common touch.

A week later, on 9 December 1936, Edward signed the Instrument of Abdication and the next day he broadcast a farewell speech to the nation. "You must believe me when I tell you that I have found it impossible to carry the heavy burden of responsibility, and to discharge my duties as King as I would wish to do, without the help and support of the woman I love." Soon Edward VIII left his country and joined Wallis Simpson in Paris. His reign had lasted 325 days, and he was now known as the Duke of Windsor.

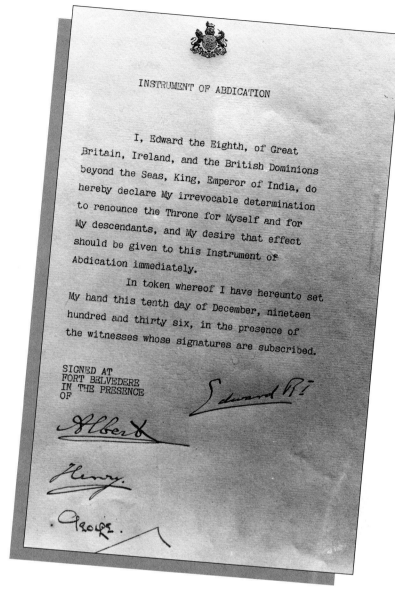

The royal family exacted its revenge on the woman who had stolen the King by denying her the title of Duchess or any other royal status. After being given some minor diplomatic posts, Edward was left to live out his life in Paris, where he had a reputation as a man who would never pick up a bill if he could avoid it. The couple met the royal family again in 1967 when they were invited to the unveiling of a commemorative plaque to Queen Mary, but relations remained strained. Edward died five years later, and the devastated Wallis went into a long-term decline, finally dying a virtual recluse in 1986. She was buried next to her husband in the royal burial place in the grounds of Windsor Castle.

ABOVE

The document of 10 December in which Edward VIII signed away the throne.

THE STAVISKY MYSTERY

Serge Alexandre Stavisky has a place in the history books as the man who brought the French to virtual civil war in 1934. Yet little is known of him, his massive swindles, or who protected him. Maybe they wanted it to stay that way.

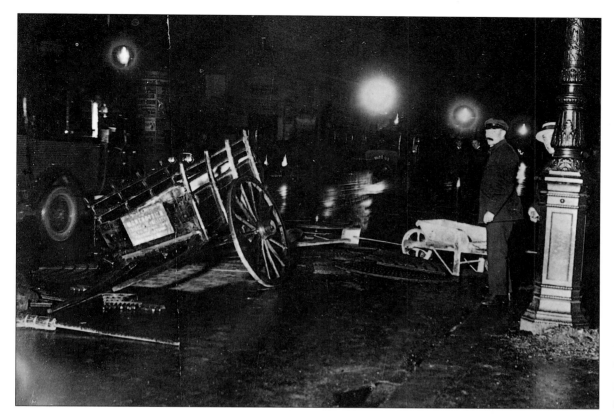

A ruined Paris barricade after a night of unrest during the Stavisky riots.

BELOW

This French cartoon evokes the sense of conspiracy and corruption that permeated l'affaire Stavisky.

The story of Serge Stavisky is both a scandal and a mystery. Why did the French government protect a major fraudster? What happened to the $18 million he swindled? Any chance of finding the answers to these questions evaporated when a bullet through the head ended his life, and, fittingly, there remains a puzzle over whether it was his or another's finger on the trigger. Whatever the answers, the legacy of this unassuming-looking man brought down two successive French governments and seriously threatened the survival of democracy in France.

Born in the Ukraine in 1888, Stavisky was a Russian Jew who emigrated to France and built up a considerable record of business disasters. The roles of café singer, night-club manager, promoter of a nude revue, manager of a soup factory, and gambling-den operator all ended in failure. Many of these jobs involved work on the periphery of the law, and perhaps it was then that Stavisky found his protective allies. Certainly he lived by the saying

RIGHT

Stavisky's wife Arlette
was a great beauty who
once won a Prix
d'Elegance at Cannes.

TUESDAY, JANUARY 9, 1934   One Penny

No. 9,398   Registered at the G.P.O.
as a Newspaper.

FIGHT TO SAVE STAVISKY'S LIFE
Hunted Banker Shoots Himself in Villa

that who you know is often more important than what you know.

Over the next few years Stavisky
succeeded in pulling off a series of
massive swindles, including the issuing
of false bonds on the security of the
municipal pawn shop in the town of
Bayonne, near Biarritz, in the deep
south west of France. It is estimated
that this unprepossessing figure made
$18 million through his trickery.

This, however, did not pass un-
noticed, and the authorities pounced
on him more than once. But Stavisky
had a first-class list of contacts, including ministers, deputies and senior

AN UNLIKELY
MASTER SWINDLER

Serge Stavisky had a pale complexion
and, it would seem, an even paler
personality. French writer Colette knew
him by sight and commented that "he
excelled at having no face". His great
passion was his wife Arlette, and he was
particularly proud that she won the Prix
d'Elegance at Cannes one year.
However, he also took a number of
mistresses for business reasons. Perhaps
fittingly for this featureless man, it is
said that his dead body held only two
pints of blood.

LES JEUX SONT FAITS

RIEN NE VA PLUS

ABOVE

The letters of Stavisky's name trample over justice and industry in this satirical cartoon of 1939.

RIGHT

Stavisky's bloodstained body can be seen at the foot of this montage from a French newspaper.

policemen. Presumably in return for bribes, they protected him, and he enjoyed virtual immunity from prosecution. When that barrier was breached and his trial began in 1927, a series of excuses for postponement held it up for seven years. Even when he was out on bail (renewed on no less than 19 occasions), he continued his complicated and illegal business activities.

Eventually the trickster was found dead from a bullet through his head. Did he fire the shot himself or did the policemen chasing him put an end to his life, to protect others? The bullet that passed through his brain ended its journey surprisingly low in the wall behind Stavisky, considering he was a tall man, but the question remains unanswered.

His death on 3 January 1934 sparked off a major scandal. Prime Minister Camille Chautemps declined to set up an inquiry into how Stavisky had maintained his immunity from prosecution for so long. (He may have known already, as his brother-in-law was head of the Paris authority which began public prosecutions.) Crowds, incited by both right wing and communist groups, rioted in the streets of Paris, and Chautemps resigned. His replacement, Edouard Daladier, dismissed the Paris prefect of police, but he too went after mass demonstrations on 6, 7 and 9 February during which 14 died.

An emergency national coalition government managed to keep the country running until the situation calmed down in November. But it was a close-run thing. A judge who claimed he held documents kept secret on the wishes of the brother-in-law of a leftist politician was found decapitated by a railway line.

Stavisky associates were tried in 1935. There were not enough chairs to accommodate everyone who wanted to watch proceedings in the packed courtroom, which heard 270 witnesses and saw the charges fill a 1,200-page Act of Accusation. Those carefully concealed facts of where the money went, and how the fraudster kept ahead of the law, remained undiscovered.

Le Petit Journal

accusée, levez-vous

et c'est le cadavre de Stavisky qui surgit devant les juges....

voir l'article

ALGER HISS, SPY OR VICTIM?

LEFT

Alger Hiss is led away to serve his five-year sentence handcuffed to a fellow prisoner keen to hide his face.

RIGHT

Communist turned spy exposer Whittaker Chambers on his way to Hiss' second trial, during 1948.

FAR RIGHT

Alger Hiss (left) shakes hands with US President Harry Truman at a UN Conference meeting in 1945.

The trial of Alger Hiss was one of the most sensational American political controversies of the twentieth century. Guilty or not, the case was a scandal. Either a man groomed for national leadership turned out to be a Russian spy, or an innocent victim was framed by the FBI (Federal Bureau of Investigation).

I n 1947 Alger Hiss was an ascending star. The Harvard graduate was a well-educated and talented lawyer and negotiator who had been closely identified with Franklin Roosevelt's "New Deal" in the 1930s. Experience in international diplomacy had brought him the honour of temporary secretary-generalship of the United Nations, and he had just become president of the Carnegie Endowment for International Peace.

Suddenly it was claimed that this talented and respected man was a spy, sending the Russians sensitive information from the highest levels of American politics. The allegations came from the mouth of Whittaker Chambers, a senior editor of *Time* magazine, and a tortured ex-communist eager to expose those with whom he had plotted in his past. Chambers was testifying before Senator Joe McCarthy's House Un-American

Activities Committee (HUAC). This was the Republican anti-communist witch-hunting committee which claimed numerous actors, politicians and officials were secretly communist plotters. These damaging allegations were often extracted from colleagues under investigation who found it expedient to name a few names to divert the spotlight away from themselves.

Hiss had known Chambers during the 1930s as George Crosley, and remembers him as a struggling free-lance journalist who was adept at sponging money and favours from all around him. Crosley's dire financial straits aroused Hiss' sympathy, and he helped him by sub-letting an apartment to him, and even providing the hapless Crosley with an old car. Eventually the thrusting young lawyer tired of Crosley's repeated lying and ended the friendship. When Chambers named him as a communist sympathizer, Hiss

claims he did not finally realize his accuser was Crosley until they were brought together at a HUAC session.

Chambers' version of events was that Hiss and several other named people were members of a communist group during the 1930s. This was a particularly damaging allegation to someone in Hiss' position, and the lawyer sued the journalist for libel.

Chambers now expanded his claims by saying that Hiss had acted as a spy for the Russians. According to him, Hiss had brought State Department documents home, had them re-typed by his wife, and passed these copies to Chambers while the originals were returned. Chambers had photographed the papers and sent them to a Russian agent. Why the originals could not have been photographed instead, saving time-consuming and possibly error-inflicting typing, was never explained by Chambers.

Further evidence was produced by Chambers after a visit to his Maryland farm, when he returned to HUAC with 35mm film stored, he claimed, in a hollowed-out pumpkin. On the film were various State Department documents. Both men were now called before a grand jury investigating these claims of espionage. Hiss denied giving Chambers documents, and was charged with perjury. (He could not be charged with espionage as the alleged offences had taken place more than three years previously, but this was what the indictment amounted to.)

If Hiss was a spy, the repercussions were endless. He had attended the post-war Yalta Conference in 1945, rubbing shoulders with Roosevelt, Stalin and Churchill. The same year he was made director of the office of special political affairs, responsible for formulating plans for the United Nations and other aspects of the peace settlement. The Russians would have benefited enormously from tip-offs about American thinking at this time, and from the other inside information that passed across Hiss' desk. Now the Cold War had set in and America feared none more than the communists, and here was an Ivy League man who had helped the enemy. If this was true, it was a major scandal.

A key piece of evidence was the typewriter on which Mrs Hiss was said to have typed the documents. The prosecution produced forensic evidence showing it was the machine on which the copies produced by Chambers were typed. Many years later Hiss established that in fact the wrong typewriter had been produced. The exhibit produced by his defence at the trial, and which the prosecution seized as proof of his guilt, did not exist when the alleged spying had taken place. Therefore the expert evidence implicating the instrument must have been fabricated.

Hiss was a key representative at the Yalta Conference where the world's major statesmen, Winston Churchill, President Franklin D. Roosevelt and Joseph Stalin, met to negotiate a lasting world peace.

NIXON'S ROLE

One of the most enthusiastic members of the HUAC forced further investigations into Alger Hiss and offered his services in defending Whittaker Chambers in his libel case. His name was Richard Nixon, and he had just entered Congress in 1948. Ever the political opportunist, Nixon rode the anti-communist bandwagon and found it took him on his own road to political success. When Alger Hiss wrote "careers have been based on my conviction", one of the careers he meant was that of the future president.

Ignorant of this, the jury at the first trial failed to reach a verdict, but a second one found Hiss guilty and on 21 January 1950 he received a five-year sentence. Alger Hiss was released on 27 November 1954, and has protested his innocence ever since.

If he was guilty, he paid a very low price for someone who had given state secrets to a foreign power. There are those on the political right who believe Hiss was guilty, and that Chambers was an American hero. Indeed in 1984 President Reagan posthumously awarded Whittaker Chambers with the Medal of Freedom, saying the ex-communist "personified the mystery of human redemption in the face of evil and suffering".

But if Chambers was lying, who helped him back up his allegations? During World War Two, the FBI used a technique of typewriter forgery in some of its counter-espionage activities. Could it be that Edgar Hoover's virulently anti-left FBI found it expedient to end the career of a liberal-minded diplomat?

ABOVE

Richard Nixon was an enthusiastic 'red' hunter who helped hunt Hiss down. Here he briefs journalists on the successes of the House Un-American Activities Committee.

THE CAMBRIDGE SPIES

LEFT

Anthony Blunt peers
balefully back at
journalists attending a
press conference held
after he was un-masked
as the 'Fourth Man'.

The Cambridge spies saga is a classic of espionage: long-term Soviet agents penetrated the British secret services, which were pathetically slow to identify them (usually after they were long gone) and tremendously keen to cover up the truth.

Daily  Mail

MONDAY, AUGUST 4, 1975

6p (CHANNEL ISLANDS 7p)

MAIL WORLD EXCLUSIVE

Philby and Blake, both now with Russian wives, meet near Moscow to talk over the legacy of their betrayal

THE TRAITORS

Imagine a film in which five elegant young men from an elite English university agree to conceal their communist sympathies, infiltrate the Establishment and work as spies. Despite the fact that the group includes notorious homosexuals, compulsive womanizers and drunken brawlers – hardly obvious spy material – they achieve their aims. One even becomes an adviser to the Queen and is knighted. The film plot would be dismissed as unbelievable. But it all happened.

Anthony Blunt, Kim Philby, Donald Maclean, Guy Burgess and John Cairncross began studies at Trinity College and Trinity Hall, at Cambridge University in England between 1926 and 1933. All were either already communists, or became heavily influenced by the Marxist economics professor Maurice Dobb (his home was known as "the red household"). Several of them were invited to join the secret and exclusive "Apostles", an intellectual and predominantly homosexual club which included some of the most brilliant students of the day. All were recruited as spies for the Soviet Union, believing that by helping this Marxist state they would further Marxist ideology and hence world peace.

Clever, idealistic, and supported by the invaluable kudos of a Cambridge education, these young men were clearly capable of achieving positions at the helm of the Establishment. The drawback was their declared communism, which attracted suspicion, so the simple thing to do was renounce their beliefs and get on with the job.

Anthony Blunt graduated in modern languages in 1932 but remained as a Cambridge don, while pursuing his keen interest in art history. Persuaded to become a spy by Burgess, he in turn recruited Maclean and Cairncross as potential agents. He then joined MI5, and throughout World War Two he passed masses of information to the Soviets. He left the secret services in 1945 to become Surveyor of the King's Pictures, but continued to supply intelligence to his controllers. This pillar of the establishment was knighted in 1956.

Harold "Kim" Philby graduated in economics and left to join an underground organization in Vienna which helped communists escape the increasingly powerful Fascists. Recruited as a spy, he returned to London in 1934, and two years later began work as a journalist writing about the Spanish Civil War. By now he pretended right-wing views, and led a risky double life as Fascist sympathizer and Soviet agent. In August 1940 he too joined MI5. His impressive reference came via the old-boy network, provided by Colonel Valentine Vivian, deputy chief of MI6, who had known Philby's father in the Indian Civil Service. He briefed the Soviets on Britain's plans for Europe after the Allied victory, and later joined MI6's counter-espionage Iberian section. Here he was able to influence British policies regarding a possible truce with Germany, working to a Soviet brief. During this time he married his second wife but continued to have numerous affairs and to drink very heavily.

Seen as a potential future head of MI6, and having been awarded a CBE (Commander of the British Empire) he was appointed station chief of MI6 in Istanbul in 1947. A posting to Washington followed two years later, involving liaison with the CIA and FBI. The Americans suspected there was an

informer working for the British, and he had a number of close shaves, but he was an excellent bluffer – he even gave a press conference in 1955 to deny spying allegations. The next year he was moved to Beirut, now posing as a journalist, and it was from here that he escaped to his Soviet masters when he heard the game was finally up. True to form, he had an affair with Maclean's wife Melinda. After his death in the Soviet Union in 1988 he was buried with full honours.

Donald Maclean was a tall and friendly figure at Cambridge whose latent homosexuality regularly emerged under the influence of alcohol. He began spying as soon as he joined the German department of the Foreign Office in 1935, and by 1938 was a diplomat at the British Embassy in Paris. Here he married a wealthy American divorcée called Melinda Marling, and the newly-weds only just managed to escape France before the German

Donald Maclean was a handsome man whose homosexual tendencies emerged when he got drunk.

Guy Francis de Moncey Burgess was a promiscuous homosexual and drunkard. Incredibly, his notoriety failed to reach MI6.

invasion. In 1944 he was appointed First Secretary at the British embassy in Washington – an excellent post for a career diplomat, and a superb one for a spy. From here he was able to pass on key information that helped the Soviets to produce their own atom bomb. Maclean was, however, a weak man who drank very heavily, and he was nearly unmasked several times. In 1949, after a spell in a senior post in Cairo, he returned to Britain for psychiatric treatment. He had become a notorious and violent drunk, perhaps because of the strain imposed by his double life. Tipped off that he was soon to be interrogated as a spy, he escaped to Moscow with Guy Burgess in 1951.

Guy Burgess earned a reputation as a hard drinker, a promiscuous homosexual (Blunt was one of his many lover) and a forthright communist while studying history at Cambridge. He suffered a nervous breakdown before his final exams and was awarded an un-

COLD WAR DOUBLE AGENTS

The dramatic rise of the Nazi Party in 1930s' Germany spurred young idealists elsewhere to adopt communism as the political theory most likely to bring about a better, and more peaceful, world. Its elegant concepts appealed to many intellectuals who were prepared to sacrifice loyalty to their country for the good of the world. The elitist Cambridge atmosphere and the necessary secrecy of practising homosexuals (who could be prosecuted for indecency) proved to be excellent training for espionage. For the Soviets, spying was just another element in a foreign policy designed to understand, and to manipulate, the actions of other states. They could not have dreamt how effective their plan to plant moles in the secret services would be.

graded degree. He visited the Soviet Union in 1934 and came back renouncing Marxism and saying that it was impossible to get drunk in Moscow. This was part of a plan hatched with Maclean to shrug off their known leftist sympathies. He built up a mixture of political, homosexual and high-society contacts which gave him access to useful information about the British, French and German governments. He joined the War Office as a propaganda expert in 1938, in a section with close links to MI6, but was sacked in 1940 (partly because he boasted of a forthcoming appointment to Moscow), after which he returned to his previous role as a producer with the British Broadcasting Corporation. He compensated for the disappointment by stepping up the excesses of his already decadent lifestyle.

Six years later he was back at the Foreign Office in a senior post advising on overseas policy, which gave him access to countless state secrets. He was reprimanded for repeated misconduct and drug-taking, and shunted around between jobs before being sent to Washington from where he sent the Soviets detailed briefings on the intricacies of American politics and US relations with its allies. He had no trouble finding lodgings in the American capital: he stayed with

Philby. Still highly undisciplined, he committed so many motoring offences that he had to return to England. By this time he was aware that his espionage might be discovered, and he fled to Moscow with Maclean.

John Cairncross moved on from Cambridge to the Treasury, and in 1942 joined Britain's most secret wartime organization, the decoding centre at Bletchley Park. He passed intercepted German messages to the Soviets via Blunt. He progressed to MI6 headquarters, specializing in German and then Yugoslavian intelligence.

The eventual exposure of the Cambridge Five came about almost despite the efforts of MI5 and MI6. It was American agents who realized that the British secret services had several highly placed moles, and who put pressure on their allies to track them down. Burgess and Maclean were tipped off and fled to their paymasters in 1951, and it took four years for the Foreign Office to admit that the pair had been Soviet agents. In 1956 the double agents held a press conference in Moscow to justify their actions. Newspaper speculation about the existence of a "third man" pointed the spotlight at Philby, prompting a Commons statement from Foreign Secretary Harold Macmillan that Philby was

Donald Maclean's wife Melinda leaves for a holiday in France. She eventually joined her husband in Moscow in 1953, and left him for Philby ten years later.

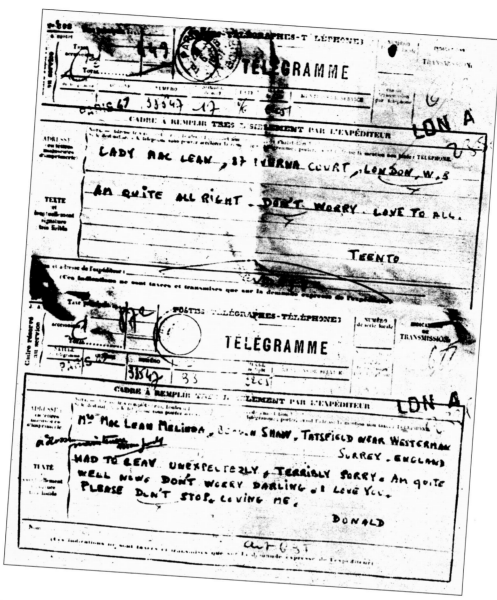

RIGHT

Reassuring telegrams to his wife from Donald Maclean after he had fled the country to avoid arrest in 1951.

innocent. He was finally exposed by the evidence of a KGB defector, but succeeded in "disappearing" to Moscow.

Blunt confessed to being a Soviet spy in 1964, and was given immunity from prosecution in return for identifying other moles. Despite this, in 1972 he became Surveyor of the Queen's Pictures. The monarch was informed that one of her advisers was a traitor, and was cautioned not to rock the boat by sacking him. He was publicly exposed in 1979, when the Palace bashfully stripped him of his knighthood. He died in 1983.

Intense speculation about a "fifth man" raised the strong suggestion that the head of MI5, Roger Hollis, was a spy, before John Cairncross was identified in 1990.

The whole affair revealed the total inadequacy of screening of staff for the secret services and of an inability to track down the traitors on the payroll. This seems mystifying considering the ringleader of the Cambridge Five, Guy Burgess, was an unstable character, a known communist in his student days, who throughout his life blurted out incriminating comments to friends, but who enjoyed the continued protection of his MI5 friends.

A story such as this makes you wonder if there was, or is, a sixth man, and a seventh, and an eighth.

THE PROFUMO AFFAIR

LEFT

The elegant Mr and Mrs John Profumo in 1960: she was a glamorous actress, he tipped as a future prime minister.

RIGHT

Ex-showgirl, lover of a British minister and a Soviet spy, Christine Keeler during her 'holiday' out of the way in Spain in March 1963.

It was a very British scandal: a blend of sex, espionage, and betrayal. A brief affair between a cabinet minister and a young good-time girl had repercussions far beyond British politics, and led to the death of the man who brought them together.

NEWS OF THE WORLD

SUNDAY, JUNE 9, 1963   EMPIRE NEWS   No. 6,239   PRICE SIXPENCE

Confessions of Christine

Six people attended the funeral of Stephen Ward in August 1963: members of his family, his girlfriend and his solicitor. Of the dozens of the high-society friends who had enjoyed his parties and used his contacts there was no sign. Ward was the sacrificial victim of the Profumo scandal that rocked Britain and exposed a secret world of vice inhabited by the very best names in society.

Ward was a successful osteopath who delighted in fun – at the simple level, practical jokes and the card game bridge, but more seriously, women, the sex lives of others, and wild parties. He built up a wide network of friends and enjoyed having and attending parties where he was able to introduce respected, established

Amusing, convivial, informal, Stephen Ward still looks somehow out of place among his besuited, society friends, who later deserted him.

Lord Astor, who rented a cottage on his estate to Stephen Ward, who used it for weekend parties.

men to young and carefree girls. Ward would often invite friends to a cottage he used in the grounds of Cliveden House, Buckinghamshire, home of Lord Astor. The fun-loving osteopath's guests would often mix with the lord's society friends.

It was on one such occasion on 8 July 1961 that Christine Keeler, who was sharing Ward's flat, met John "Jack"

Profumo, Secretary of State for War in the Conservative government. Profumo had become an MP at the age of 25, and had risen to a senior government post. Some tipped him as a future prime minister, although they commented that to achieve that he would have to tame his love of night-life. Keeler was a pretty, copper-haired 18-year-old with little experience of the world, who was working as a topless showgirl at Soho's Cabaret Club. She was cavorting naked by a swimming pool when Lord Astor arrived with some of his guests, including the Profumos. Mrs Profumo lent her a swimsuit.

The minister and the showgirl were soon sleeping together, and Profumo gave her a number of "gifts" (including a cigarette lighter and money for her mother) to pay for her services. Barely a month had passed when the minister was advised by a colleague to end the affair. He risked exposure, he was warned, besides which the spy service MI5 had its eye on Ward and felt he could be indiscreet. The muttered

Christine Keeler told her story to a newspaper as the Profumo affair blew up.

Sunday Mirror
AND SUNDAY PICTORIAL

5d.   June 9, 1963 No. 10

PROFUMO: HIS LETTER TO CHRISTINE

9/8/81

Darling,

In great haste & because I can get no reply from your phone—

Alas something's blown up tomorrow night & I can't therefore make it. I'm terribly sorry especially as I leave the next day for various trips & then a holiday so won't be able to see you again until some time in September. Blast it. Please take great care of yourself & don't run away.

Love J.

I'm writing this 'cos I know you're off for the day tomorrow & I want you to know before you go if I still can't reach you by phone.

FOR some months a rumour has been buzzing around Those In The Know about a letter written by the Right Honourable John Dennis Profumo, Privy Councillor.

[A Privy Councillor is one of the Queen's "right trusty and well beloved" advisers.]

Mr. Profumo was the Tory Secretary of State for War until the British public studied their newspapers on Thursday morning.

According to the rumour Mr. Profumo's letter was addressed to Miss Christine Keeler, who no longer needs to be introduced or described to anybody who isn't blind or deaf.

Rumour Correct

It has also been said that The Letter was, or had been, in the possession of a national newspaper.

Today the Sunday Mirror can emphatically state:

1 The rumour is correct.

2 The letter was written by Mr. John Profumo.

3 It was addressed to Miss Christine Keeler and began with the word "Darling." It was signed: "Love, J."

Now that the War Minister has resigned after confessing an association with Christine Keeler, it is possible to explain why this letter was not published, and precisely what happened to it.

In January, after a shooting incident at the West End flat of Dr. Stephen Ward, Miss Keeler, a model from Staines, who was then 20, was in touch with the Sunday Pictorial

concerning her story of how she had been involved in the society life of London.

During the talks with a Pictorial reporter she alleged that among the men with whom she had had affairs were Mr. John Profumo and a Russian diplomat serving in London—Captain Eugene Ivanov.

Miss Keeler produced a letter Mr. Profumo had written to her in 1961.

Now that Mr. Profumo is the centre of a grave political scandal, and now he has confessed to the impropriety of his association with Miss Keeler, THAT LETTER IS REPRODUCED ON THIS PAGE TODAY.

But for two very sound reasons the Editor of the Sunday Pictorial decided at the time not to publish the letter or to publish Christine Keeler's story:

● The Editor was not satisfied that this letter constituted evidence of any substantial nature. It was effusive but not conclusive.

● Publication of the letter might have ruined the public career of a Minister on "evidence" from a young woman who clearly would not have produced the letter if Mr. Profumo's interests were uppermost in her consideration.

Not Disclosed

The existence of the letter was not disclosed to the public. Miss Christine Keeler's story was not published.

Dr. Stephen Ward, who was arrested by two Scotland Yard officers yesterday, offered to writ· a story himself, and his article—entitled "My Friendship with Christine"—appeared in the Sunday Pictorial on March 17.

Dr. Ward referred to Mr. Profumo's letter, published on this page today, in an interview with the Daily Telegraph two days ago.

THE FACTS ARE:

● Miss Keeler herself had not asked for the return of Mr. Profumo's letter.

● The letter was never discussed during Dr. Ward's negotiations with the Sunday

Turn to Back Page

What the letter said:

9-8-61

Darling,

In great haste and because I can get no reply from your phone—

Alas something's blown up tomorrow night and I can't therefore make it. I'm terribly sorry especially as I leave the next day for various trips and then a holiday so won't be able to see you again until some time in September. Blast it Please take great care of yourself and don't run away.

Love J.

I'm writing this 'cos I know you're off for the day tomorrow and I want you to know before you go if I still can't reach you by phone.

words amounted to a clear warning: stay clear of her or you could be in trouble. Profumo stopped seeing Keeler towards the end of the year.

What he was not told was that Keeler had apparently also been seeing another friend of Ward's, Russian spy Captain Eugene Ivanov.

A year later a shooting incident at Ward's London flat provided the catalyst for the scandal to come into the open. Keeler had been seeing two West Indian men, Aloyius "Lucky" Gordon and Johnny Edgecombe. The rivals had fought over her in October, and Edgecombe faced assault charges. Infuriated that Keeler intended to give evidence against him, Edgecombe turned up at the flat (which in the meantime Keeler had left, but was by chance visiting that day) on 14 December. Refused entry, he fired a few pistol shots at the door in frustration. Terrified neighbours in the select mews buildings called the police.

The press picked up on the incident, and Keeler, thrown into the limelight, started to blurt out parts of a story of sexual intrigue and an affair with a top politician. Ward was appalled and their previously close relationship with him cast as the brother/father figure became strained. While he loved decadence, he was acutely aware of the importance of keeping the activities of his friends out of the public eye. By the time Edgecombe's case came to court in March 1963 his ex-girlfriend was unable to give evidence because she had been spirited away to Spain.

The mysterious disappearance of a woman who was rumoured to have been having an affair with the Minister for War only fuelled speculation. The matter was raised in Parliament, and on 22 March Profumo rose to make a statement to MPs in the House of Commons. "My wife and I first met Miss Keeler at a house party in July 1961, at Cliveden. Among a number of people there was Dr Stephen Ward, whom we already knew slightly, and a Mr Ivanov, who was an attaché at the

ABOVE

Mandy Rice-Davies shared Christine Keeler's lifestyle and some of her lovers, and helped to spill the beans.

A VERY PUBLIC TRIAL

The two key prosecution witnesses at the trial were Christine Keeler and Mandy Rice-Davies. Both had lived at Ward's flat at some time and had been part of his set. Both had received money from men in return for sex, and they had teamed up to provide group sex sessions. They had given money to Ward, but he had often loaned them more than these small sums, and had allowed them to live rent free. Their evidence was damaging, but did not show Ward to be their pimp. Only one of the men they were alleged to have had sex with appeared as a witness. The trial developed into an attack on Ward's morality, on a promiscuous and sexually active way of life. This had a strong impact on the jury, as did Judge Justice Sir Archibald Marshall's obvious dislike for much of what he heard. The Establishment got its scapegoat.

Russian Embassy." MPs were hanging on his every word as he continued: "Between July and December 1961 I met Miss Keeler on about half a dozen occasions at Dr Ward's flat when I called to see him and his friends", he told the fascinated house. "Miss Keeler and I were on friendly terms. There was no impropriety whatsoever in my acquaintance with Miss Keeler."

Profumo left to the echoing cheers of relieved Conservative MPs, but he had committed one of the greatest sins possible for a British politician: he had lied to the House of Commons. In many ways this, and not the affair, was to be the cause of his downfall. Public interest increased in the story of a minister's affair, spiced up with the possibility of a spying connection. Ten weeks later, Profumo resigned.

Meanwhile, the Establishment decided that the true villain of the Profumo scandal was Stephen Ward. He was to be prosecuted for receiving money from prostitutes. Now it was Ward who blinked into the television lights, while Profumo, ex-minister, pondered his regrets in private. The security organisation MI5, which had been keen to trap Ivanov and get him to pass secrets or defect, and had been

kept informed by Ward of the exploits of both Profumo and Ivanov, now did its own disappearing act. The trial itself was a farce and it was clear from the judge's summing up that Stephen Ward would be found guilty.

Ward took an overdose of sleeping pills on the night of 30 July, and died four days later.

John Profumo is now a rich business-man who has worked tremendously hard to help alcoholics, drug addicts and the homeless in the East End of London. A successful film made in 1989 told the story to a new generation, and ensured his name will always be synonymous with a scandal of the early 1960s.

The Profumo affair might have made fewer headlines in another time: the involvement of a Russian spy came at the height of the Cold War, and the more relaxed sexual morals of the swinging sixties had not yet become established. Ward was no pimp, but the people he thought of as friends let him become a scapegoat. On the espionage side, the Profumo Affair showed the British security services in a very poor light and damaged Britain's relationships with its allies, particularly the appalled Americans.

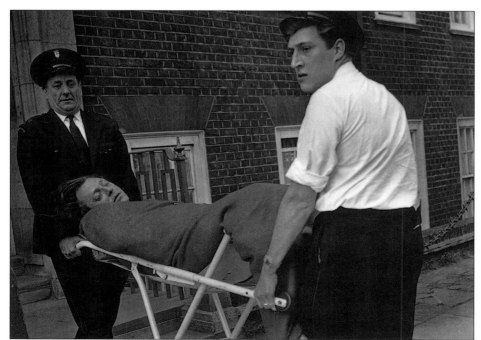

Stephen Ward is taken into St Stephen's Hospital after his overdose. He never woke up.

SENATOR KENNEDY
and the drowned girl

Chappaquiddick is the scandal that won't go away. Edward Kennedy's evasive behaviour after a fatal accident has haunted his political career, and probably blocked his path to the White House.

It was a noisy party. A neighbour remembers that the singing, laughter and general hell-raising continued until one o'clock in the morning. Senator Edward Kennedy, then 37, was hosting a reunion party for five other men and six women from his brother Bobby's 1968 campaign team. They were there to celebrate . . .

At 8am on Saturday, 19 July 1969, the police chief of Edgartown, Dominick Arena, drew up in his car at Poucha Pond bridge, where fishermen had spotted an upturned car in the water. When he phoned into his office to check on the licence plate he got a surprise: plate L78 207 belonged to Senator Edward Kennedy. Arena feared that his scuba diver would find the politician's body in the sunken Oldsmobile. Instead, the diver emerged with the corpse of a woman.

Kennedy presented himself at Edgartown police station at 10am, saying he was the driver of the car, and his friend US attorney Paul Markham then drafted a bland statement about the incident. Economical with the truth as it was, the statement showed a US senator admitting to a wait of 10 hours before reporting a fatal accident. That delay lies at the heart of the Chappaquiddick scandal. Kennedy's actions and demeanour have been closely examined, and found wanting.

There are those who believe that the time-lapse was partly spent in trying to get the man who had organized the party to take responsibility. Lawyer Joe Gargan was Edward Kennedy's first cousin, and a key aide. He organized a number of reunions for the close-knit team which had worked on Bobby Kennedy's 1968 presidential campaign. The office was known as the "boiler room", and the six women on the team were known as the "boiler-room girls". They and other staff had transferred their loyalties to Ted after his brother's assassination in June of that year. Edward himself had been shaken by the murder, and had drunk heavily, driven recklessly, and chased women even more eagerly during the last year.

BELOW

The death car: Kennedy's Oldsmobile after it was hauled out of the river with Mary Jo Kopechne's body inside.

LEFT

Edward Kennedy making a speech to support a fellow Democrat. Without Chappaquiddick, he might have been speaking as the President.

Gargan had arranged the party at Lawrence Cottage on Chappaquiddick Island, which is near Cape Cod and is separated from a larger island, Martha's Vineyard, by a 150 metre channel. A ferry made regular crossings from the main town of Edgartown, the last one leaving at midnight, and motel rooms had been booked in Edgartown on this occasion.

Festivities were in full swing when Kennedy left with Mary Jo Kopechne at some time after 11.15pm. The senator took the keys to his black Oldsmobile 88 because his part-time chauffeur Joe Crimmins was too drunk to drive. Kennedy later claimed he intended to take Mary Jo for the last ferry, but there is some confusion as to what time he left, and it may already have been too late to catch the boat. Furthermore, Mary Jo did not take her handbag with her, or ask Esther Newberg for the key

to the motel room they were sharing. Were the senator and the boiler-room girl going to drive somewhere private to make love?

Local deputy sheriff Christopher Look was passing near the scene of the party at about 12.40am. A large black car with a licence plate beginning with L7 and ending in a 7 passed him, turned into an unpaved road, then rapidly reversed out as if the driver had realized his mistake, and sped off down Dike Road. This leads away from the ferry connection on Chappaquiddick, and towards the Poucha Pond bridge. Perhaps the driver of the car spotted Look's police car and was alarmed at the prospect of being stopped.

Whether or not this was the vehicle carrying Mary Jo Kopechne and Edward Kennedy – and there is little doubt that it was – the senator's car failed to cross the narrow, angled

Mary Jo Kopechne, left, and the other "boiler-room girls" during a 1967 staff meeting with Senator Robert F. Kennedy.

bridge, and dived into the swiftly running water, landing upside-down. A strong swimmer, Kennedy managed to get out and then looked around for Mary Jo. Realizing she was trapped in the car, he dived repeatedly into the strong current to search for her, but to no avail.

So far, we have a tragedy and the possibility of some impropriety, but no scandal. This is where the story takes a strange twist. For the drenched man now walked the mile back to the cottage, ignoring an unmanned rescue station with a burning red light, and several houses with their lights still on. Reaching the cottage, Kennedy slumped into a car and called out for Gargan and Markham. He explained what had happened and they drove back to the bridge, where they fought the current and the darkness of the cold waters in a series of unsuccessful bids to find Mary Jo. By now it was clear she could not have survived.

Kennedy's colleagues told him to contact the police and a lawyer but he was distraught and confused, and did not follow their advice. They drove him to the other side of the island, and saw him set off to swim across to Edgartown. Once there he walked to his hotel, the Shiretown Inn, changed out of his sodden clothes, and rested. He later came out of his room, bumping into the hotel manager. Kennedy asked the time and was told it was 2.25am. He appeared perfectly calm as he returned to his room.

Gargan and Markham got to the hotel just after 8am the next day. They found a well-groomed Edward Kennedy chatting with fellow-guests on the terrace. An argument ensued when they realized he had still not reported the incident to the police, and Kennedy suggested they find a quiet place from which to phone his lawyer and his Washington office. The three men took the ferry to Chappaquiddick and Kennedy began dialling from the phone near the ferry landing. Gargan spotted the ferry returning to the island with a

HOW DID MARY JO DIE?

A crucial question to Chappaquiddick is how Mary Jo Kopechne died. Did she drown in the dark waters, or did she find a pocket of air and perish only when that oxygen ran out? If the latter was the case, could she have been saved if better help had been called immediately? The scuba diver who found her body said the face was pushed into the footwell, the hands clutching the back seat. In an overturned car filling with water, that is where air could have been trapped. An autopsy would have solved the query, but a Kennedy aide helped in getting the body whisked away on Sunday. Mary Jo was buried the following Tuesday, and her body was never exhumed.

The Kennedy family in 1937, when Joseph Kennedy was US Ambassador to Britain. He and his wife are seated in armchairs. At the back are (left to right) John F Kennedy, Robert and Rosemary Kennedy, and seated are Patricia, Jean, Eunice, Kathleen, Edward and Joseph Junior.

THE KENNEDY DYNASTY

Edward Kennedy was part of a family closely identified with liberal politics and tragedy. He was a son of the American industrialist and diplomat Joseph Patrick Kennedy. His brother John F Kennedy had risen to be president of the USA when he was assassinated in Dallas in 1963. Five years later Bobby Kennedy was a civil rights campaigner and was pursuing the presidential nomination in 1968 when he was murdered in Los Angeles.

tow-truck, and assumed, correctly, that the car had been found. Kennedy then finally went to the police.

He answered few questions, preferring to submit the statement drafted with Markham, and was then swept off back to the Kennedy family home a few miles up the coast at Hyannis Port.

Bewildered at the incident, and a little intimidated by the Kennedy reputation, Arena made no objection to this, and did not insist on having his own questions answered. Instead, he found he was giving answers to some of the reports who had got a whiff of the story and begun to descend on Chappaquiddick. They wanted to know what sort of party Kennedy had been hosting, where he had been going with Mary Jo, whether his driving had been reckless, why he had not called for a rescue team, and why he had delayed telling the police about the incident. These are not questions a potential president can survive having asked of him.

Mary Jo Kopechne was buried in Pennsylvania the next Tuesday. Edward Kennedy attended the funeral wearing a neck brace – the only time anyone saw him in one – although he never claimed to have injuries from the accident. Perhaps his advisers suggested this would inspire some sympathy from a public which was increasingly critical of Kennedy's behaviour.

Those powerful aides ensures a prompt court hearing that Friday, at which Kennedy pleaded guilty to leaving the scene of an accident. The world's media had gathered for a spectacle, but within seven minutes Kennedy had been given a suspended two-year sentence and was out of the building. That night he made a television address carried on three national networks. He denied having been drunk, acting immorally, but admitted "I regarded as indefensible the fact that I did not report the accident to the police immediately". The public received the impression of a callous man behaving dishonestly. Chappaquiddick was not going to go away.

The District Attorney began a new investigation into the accident, and an inquest was held behind closed doors on 5 January 1970. Those present felt Kennedy was able to duck questions on inconsistencies in his evidence, sometimes with the help of Judge Boyle. The judge's report emerged 16 weeks later, and made damning read-ing for Kennedy. Judge Boyle declined to believe that the original destination of the fateful journey was the ferry, and concluded that "his turn onto Dike Road was intentional". Kennedy was familiar with the island, and therefore with the angled bridge. "If Kennedy knew of this hazard, his operation of the vehicle constituted criminal conduct," wrote the judge. "Finally, I find there is probable cause to believe that Edward M Kennedy operated his motor vehicle negligently, and appears to have contributed to the death of Mary Jo Kopechne." The judgement confirmed the public view that Kennedy had left a wild party with a girl intending to have sex on the beach, that his reckless driving led to an accident, and that he then tried to save his reputation rather than get help.

Chappaquiddick killed Edward Kennedy's chances of winning future presidential campaigns, for whenever he had a sniff of the Democratic nomination, the same old questions would come up again. He continued to be a powerful liberal spokesman, but he could have been President of the United States.

LEFT

Senator Kennedy leaving court on 25 July 1969 after pleading guilty to charge of leaving the scene of an accident.

TED'S PAST: BRIBES, LIES & COWARDICE

THE DISAPPEARING MP

When John Stonehouse disappeared off a Miami beach the obituary writers primed themselves to do the British politician justice. Then he was sensationally found living under a false identity in Australia, and tragedy became scandal.

In Frederick Forsyth's novel *The Day of the Jackal*, the main character obtains a false identity by applying for a passport in the name of a dead man who would now be about his age. All he needs to do is get a copy of the man's birth certificate, fill in the forms, and wait. Forsyth is renowned for his thorough research, and a number of people have copied his simple method. John Stonehouse was a Forsyth fan.

Born into a family of modest means in 1925, Stonehouse was always something of an idealist and decided quite early on that he wanted to go into politics. First, though, he went out to Africa at the age of 25 with his young family, and earned a reputation as a campaigner for black causes. He returned to Britain an acknowledged expert on the African continent, and became an MP in 1957.

Twelve years on, the rising star was appointed Minister of State for Aviation, a post quickly widened to Minister of State for Technology, and he then gained a promotion to Postmaster General. However, Stonehouse could be autocratic and some rivals resented his rapid rise, and when Labour lost the 1970 election, he was left out of the shadow cabinet.

Suddenly left with only his MP's salary, Stonehouse needed another source of income, and set up an export consultancy company and various other businesses. In 1972 he came across a chance to expand his foreign commercial activities in a way which also satisfied his wish to help Third World causes. He had been interested in the problems of Bangladesh, a poor substate of Pakistan, for a number of years, and was a trustee of The Bangladesh Fund and an honorary citizen of the country. Now it was proposed that he build a bridge between Great Britain and Bangladesh, in the form of the British Bangladesh Trust. It was hoped this would evolve into a bank which could serve British Bengali immigrants, and foster trade links.

THE OTHER WOMAN

Sheila Buckley became secretary to John Stonehouse in 1968. Four years later, after she had divorced her husband, MP and aide became lovers. She claimed she knew nothing of his bizarre escape plan, but she did travel out to join him in Australia after he was discovered. They showed each other a loyalty that neither found in the rest of their lives. He divorced his wife and married his former secretary in 1981.

The launch was a disaster, when the news-sheet aimed at attracting Bengali shareholders was found to have broken various technical rules. Investors balked at putting money into an already tainted scheme, and as it struggled for life it was hit by the banking crisis of 1973.

Stonehouse's career was in a mess. Politically he was too far right of central thinking of the Labour Party, commercially he was marked as at best naive. The frustrated idealist decided to make a new start. Over a two-year period he obtained loans of £729,500 ($1.9 million) for his companies on his personal guarantee. He also found the names of two constituents of his age who had recently died, Joseph Markham and Clive Mildoon. He interviewed their widows to check if they had ever applied for passports. As they had not, he could do so using their names. Using copies of their birth certificates he applied for passports, with his photograph verified in one case by that of a fellow MP, Neil McBride, who died at about this time. Stonehouse then transferred a large proportion of the loaned money to Australian and Swiss banks. He also took out a number

of life insurance policies to provide for his wife and family.

Equipped with two false identities and with access to a small fortune, Stonehouse was ready for his flight to a new life. He achieved this very simply. On 20 November 1974, during a business trip to Florida with a colleage, he left his clothes in a beach hut, went swimming off a Miami beach, and vanished.

Stonehouse's sudden disappearance prompted speculation in Britain that the Mafia, or perhaps one of his other many enemies, had killed him. Meanwhile Stonehouse had reached Australia via Honolulu, and was busy introducing himself at various banks as Mr Markham and Mr Mildoon, completing the transfer of funds from the other side of the world. Unfortunately a bank clerk noticed that he had seen the same tall Englishman at two banks introducing himself by different names, and told the police.

The police thought the Englishman with the complicated finances could be Lord Lucan, who had recently disappeared after allegedly murdering the family nanny. Interpol identified

LEFT

The family he left behind. Wife Barbara Stonehouse with son Matthew and daughter Jane waiting in vain for the MP at Heathrow airport.

THE AFTERMATH

After his release from jail, Stonehouse had some success as a writer of thrillers, and talked much of the past with a diminishing band of friends. He never felt he had done wrong: "Whatever I was accused of, it was purely internal transactions within my own companies," he said. Treated as a figure of curiosity, he appeared on a number of TV shows. During filming of one such programme in 1988, he collapsed and later died. No politician sent flowers to his funeral.

him as the missing MP, and Stonehouse was picked up on Christmas Eve. After failed attempts to obtain sanctuary in seven countries (including Bangladesh) Stonehouse eventually travelled back to Britain voluntarily. On 24 April 1976 his trial began on 21 charges of theft, fraud and deception. He took over his defence himself, claiming that he felt John Stonehouse had become a humbug and a fraud, and that he wanted to live his life as he really was – which required the change of identity. He failed to convince the jury that this was sufficient defence, and was found guilty of most of the charges, being sentenced to seven years. His secretary, Sheila Buckley, got a suspended term of two years.

It is a truism of British politics that if an MP is involved in a scandal, it will centre around sex if he is a Conservative, and money if he is a Labour man, on the basis that few Conservatives have serious financial difficulties anyway. This is born out by the Stonehouse case, but what was truly scandalous was the way a respected politician planned and achieved his disappearance when life took a twist for the worse.

WATERGATE

Only one American President has been forced to resign before being impeached: Richard Nixon for his part in Watergate, probably the world's greatest political scandal.

Early on the morning of 17 June 1972, five intruders were caught by the police on the sixth floor of the Watergate complex, home of the Democratic National Committee which was in the throes of fighting the 1972 presidential campaign. The incident did not attract much attention, and the Republican President Nixon was returned to office in the poll. But the seeds of his downfall had been sown. Most of the credit for the unravelling of this complex story goes to the *Washington Post*, which dug away at the mystery despite the derision which greeted some of its stories.

Nixon faces the cameras after agreeing to finally release some of the material demanded during the impeachment probe.

Members of the Senate Watergate investigation committee hard at work unravelling the story. Left to right: Senators Lowell Weicker, Edward Gurney, Howard Baker, and Sam Ervin, counsel Samuel Dash, and Senators Herman Talmadge, Daniel Inouye, and Joseph Montoya.

The five men arrested early that June morning were: James McCord, who had been an FBI agent and chief of the CIA's Physical Security Division; Bernard Baker, an ex-CIA agent; Virgilio Gonzalez, a locksmith; Eugenio Martinez, who like Gonzalez was an exiled Cuban; and Frank Sturgis; a former US Marine. This team was hardly made up of your average small-time burglars, especially as none was from the Washington area. It emerged that the burglary had been funded by the Committee for the re-election of the President (CRP, or CREEP), a Republican campaigning organization. A central figure in charge of the CRP's "dirty tricks" fund was John Mitchell, once US Attorney-General, now Nixon's campaign manager.

None of this hampered the re-election of Richard Nixon with running mate Spiro Agnew in the 1972 election. Rather conveniently, the trial of the Watergate burglars and two of their paymasters (Gordon Liddy and Howard Hunt) had been scheduled for the following January. It was rumoured that the "Watergate Seven" had been promised "executive clemency" if Judge John Sirica sent them to jail. When the trial began, it was clear that they might need it. Hunt changed his plea to guilty, but others pleaded ignorance of the source of their funding, claiming money had simply arrived through the post in envelopes for them.

It was obvious that a cover-up was being attempted, and in February a Senate Investigation Committee was

John Ehrlichman arrives for his trial on charges relating to Watergate. He was once Nixon's top domestic advisor.

appointed to investigate wrongdoing during the presidential campaign. While it was sitting, the American press was revealing that the FBI and the CIA had been involved in the Watergate break-in and subsequent attempts to keep it quiet, on instructions from the White House. Nixon's denials of any involvement by him or his staff began to appear either disingenuous or an admission of incompetence. James McCord also produced evidence of attempts to block the investigation in

THE PLUMBERS

The "plumbers" were born after the New York Times revealed files from the "Pentagon papers" containing damaging information about America's involvement in the Vietnam War. A Special Investigations Unit was set up to stop and trace the leaks, hence the jokey nickname, the plumbers. Soon its brief had widened to include just about any activity which would discredit those who challenged the president. Bugging, wire-tapping, surveillance, and thefts were carried out by a staff of 50 under the head of the unit, Agil Krogh Jr, working from room 216 in the Executive Office building next door to the White House.

return for a lighter sentence.

Aware of the danger of his position, Nixon decided to sacrifice two of his aides. On 30 April 1973 he addressed the nation, acknowledging that there had been a cover-up – "an effort to conceal the facts from the public, from you and from me" – and announcing the resignation of Bob Haldeman (chief of staff) and John Ehrlichman (chief adviser on domestic affairs). In a statement astonishing for its hypocrisy, he added: "The easiest course would be for me to blame those to whom I delegated the responsibility to run the campaign. But that would be a cowardly thing to do. In any organization, the man at the top must bear the responsibility. I accept it."

Six weeks later one of Haldeman's aides told the Senate Investigation Committee that Nixon had secretly tape-recorded his conversations in the White House since 1971. Here was the chance to find out if the President had known burglaries and other crimes were being committed for his benefit. Nixon desperately tried to stall handing over the tapes, pleading executive

Bob Haldeman is sworn in before testifying to the Senate Watergate committee.

NIXON ADMITS HE HID FACTS

Tried to Bar FBI Gate Probe; He Expects to Be Impeached; 'Resign' Demands Rise in GOP

"...Those arguing my case, as well as those passing judgment on the case, did so with information that was incomplete and in some respects erroneous. This was a serious act of omission for which I take full responsibility and which I deeply regret.

"...It [is] clear that portions of the tapes of these June 23 conversations are at variance with certain of my previous statements."
—President Nixon

privilege, and offering summaries of their contents. His lawyers also pointed out that there were inexplicable gaps in the tapes, one of more than 18 minutes during a conversation with Haldeman three days after the Watergate break-in. The tape of a crucial meeting with John Dean, the White House counsel, was also missing. Nixon's credibility hit rock bottom, and people began to look into the mechanism for impeaching a President.

It took almost a year for the courts to obtain most of the tapes, by which time the burglars were serving jail sentences, and Haldeman, Ehrlichman, Mitchell and others had pleaded guilty to, or been charged with offences related to Watergate. Apart from various revelations in the tapes, the public was appalled at the foul language of the President, and the phrase "expletive deleted" became an international joke. At the end of July 1974 the impeachment process began, boosted by Nixon's admission that he had taken steps to divert the FBI's Watergate investigation away from the White House. On 8 August in a tearful speech, Nixon resigned the presidency before the shame of impeachment. He made no admission of guilt, but said he deeply regretted "any injuries that might have been done". A month later his successor, Gerald Ford, granted him an unconditional pardon, allowing the disgraced former president to avoid trial for perjury.

It is a mark of the significance of Watergate that just about any political scandal since has been given a tag with "-gate" on the end, carrying with it implications of megalomania, paranoia, and immorality. Watergate lessened America's respect for the role of president that Nixon had so abused. It also showed that in a democracy, corruption and crime even at the very top can be exposed and punished. Ironically it also showed that crime can pay, for many of those involved in Watergate made their fortunes from books about the scandal.

DE LOREAN'S DREAM CAR

John De Lorean succeeded in obtaining $160 million from the British government to finance a factory which would build his dream car. The deal proved disastrous for everybody except De Lorean, who showed a remarkable talent for feathering his own nest.

John De Lorean was a hero to Belfast, Northern Ireland, in 1979. The sleek American businessman had opened a car plant at which more than 1,500 people worked in a city riven by strife and unemployment. He was everything you would expect of a Detroit car manufacturer: dressed in expensive suits, accompanied by glamorous women, and prone to shooting from the hip. His background was impressive: in 1972 at the age of 47 he had reached the heights of executive vice-president of General Motors, the American motor giant. Then he had left – criticizing his ex-employer for its "lack of moral decision-making" – and after several successful years as a consultant, founded his own company to make the car he believed the world deserved. A master of public relations, De Lorean remained something of a darling to the press, and was able to attract new investors for the exciting car to be produced by his De Lorean Motor Company (DMC).

In the summer of 1978, the firm was looking for a site from which to mass-produce the vehicle. The Puerto Ricans had offered an excellent support package if the car were to be made in their country, and the deal was almost settled when a call came from the Northern Ireland Development Association (NIDA). This had been set up by Britain's Labour government to attract industry to Northern Ireland, which was blighted by lack of investment and years of violent unrest. The NIDA offer was generous: $97 million, a third of it as a straight grant, while another $20 million need not be repaid if certain employment targets were achieved. This was too good to miss, and the deal was signed on 3 August 1978.

De Lorean promised that he would transform green fields into a sophisticated car plant, and untrained hands into skilled workers who would produce an innovative vehicle within 20 months. In hindsight, it seems incredible that no one doubted his claims. But governments are peopled by bureaucrats, not businessmen.

De Lorean used to boast that he drew no salary from DMC. This was true, but it did not mean his efforts went unrewarded. He was paid a six-figure retainer plus massive expenses that supported a lavish globetrotting lifestyle and an opulent New York apartment. Even this was not enough for De Lorean. In a scheme which remains a mystery to this day, he arranged for multi-million dollar payments to be made to the Swiss bank account of a Panama-registered company known as GDP Services. De Lorean claimed this company helped with design development, but others are not so sure. De Lorean also negotiated an additional $33 million loan from NIDA, and bank loans for $40 million, guaranteed by the Northern Ireland Department of Commerce. He achieved this with bluster and threats to pull out of Belfast – knowing that the Northern Ireland authorities were terrified of losing their prestigious tenant.

Production of the new car was beset with problems and the 20-month deadline was nine months past when on 21 January 1981 John De Lorean displayed his brainchild to the motoring press. The De Lorean-12 looked impressive: a sleek grey sports car with futuristic gull-wing doors. When it was shipped over to America, it attracted queues of buyers prepared to part with $25,000 for it. De Lorean appeared to have achieved all he had promised, and he began planning a restructuring and flotation of DMC that would net him millions of dollars and reduce the British government's holding.

Then everything began to go horribly wrong. The car was so badly put together that each De Lorean had virtually to be rebuilt in America, and customers were soon returning with lists of faults. Those eye-catching doors, in particular, had the unfortunate habit of jamming, trapping the irate driver at the wheel. A year on, DMC's car pounds were packed with cars it could not sell. The press began to look at the financial side of DMC, too, and unearthed GPD and other mysteries.

The beginning of the end came in September 1981 when De Lorean's secretary, Marian Gibson, decided to spill the beans and tipped off a British MP and later the British press. Nothing came out in public, but the alarmed government instigated its own investigations and quickly realized that DMC was disintegrating at some speed. It began wrangling with De Lorean, demanding that he put up some of his money to keep the ailing firm going. De Lorean stalled, and his behaviour became eccentric and he began taking

ABOVE

The futuristic De Lorean features in the Spielberg movie *Back to the Future II*.

OPPOSITE LEFT

De Lorean and his wife Christine Ferrare leave Los Angeles Federal Court after the first day of his trial for conspiring to distribute drugs.

THE MOVIE-STAR CAR

The futuristic lines of the De Lorean 12 made it the natural car for Michale J Fox to drive in the movie Back to the Future. John De Lorean showed his acumen through an agreement with Universal Studios that he receive five per cent of profits on sales of a miniature version of the car sold to children. The British government which funded development and manufacture of the original car was not included in the deal.

advice from a psychic, known only as Sonja.

The final chapter of this saga takes a bizarre twist. An old friend of De Lorean's, James Hoffman, had agreed to help the Federal Drug Enforcement Agency rather than go to prison for drugs offences. While setting up a "sting" to trap a cocaine smuggler called William Hetrick, it was agreed that Hoffman would try to pull De Lorean in too. On 18 October 1982, De Lorean was secretly filmed receiving packages of drugs in the Sheraton La Reina Hotel, Los Angeles, and arrested by the FBI. DMC's Belfast plant was shut

down the same day.

Now De Lorean was able to use some of the millions he had acquired to hire a superb criminal defence lawyer, Howard Weitzman. Having succeeded in delaying the trial until April 1984, Weitzman discredited the prosecution witnesses in the box, and argued that the FBI had set out to entrap De Lorean. There is a wonderful irony in that a man who had duped a whole government was now presented as a victim of "Big Brother." It worked, and De Lorean walked free. He became a born-again Christian, and was later acquitted of fraud charges.

GOD'S
WHEELER-DEALER

RIGHT

Roberto Calvi has a
haunted look as he
enters a Milan court for
his money-export trial
in May 1981.

A body hanging under a bridge spanning
London's River Thames brought global
attention to an extraordinary Italian banking
scandal which linked massive fraud with
Freemasonry, the Vatican and the Mafia.

I can prove that my husband was murdered

Huge crowds regularly fill St Peter's Square to celebrate Mass and see the Pope. But behind the impressive edifice lurked a secret world.

Roberto Calvi's lifeless corpse was spotted hanging from Blackfriars Bridge in London on the morning of Friday, 18 June 1982. His pockets were filled with bricks and banknotes, mainly dollars and lire. It was a sensational twist in an extraordinary tale of corruption, deceit and murder.

The story begins with Michele Sindona, a Sicilian financier known for his links with the Vatican bank and the Mafia – who for different reasons preferred a shroud of secrecy to surround their activities. Flamboyant and charming, he was the opposite of the earnest, intense Calvi when they met in Milan in the late 1960s. However, they shared an interest in complex financial dealings, and could be of use to each other in furthering their considerably ambitions. Calvi controlled a large bank called Ambrosiano, which meant he had access to capital. Sindona had superb contacts and expertise in evading Italian banking laws by setting up foreign companies through which money could be laundered.

Calvi was born into a Catholic family in Milan in 1920, and was a fine linguist by the time he joined the Ambrosiano Bank at the age of 26. He rose through the ranks quickly because of his skill at devising money-making and money-moving schemes in which, metaphorically, side and back doors were used more often than main entrances. His unwillingness to give direct answers to questions was tolerated because he made the bank a lot of money. He became chairman in November 1975.

At around this time he joined an order of Freemasons called P2 (Propaganda Two) headed by Lucio Gelli. This sinister and secretive group included members of the judiciary, government and numerous other influential organizations and was a hotbed of

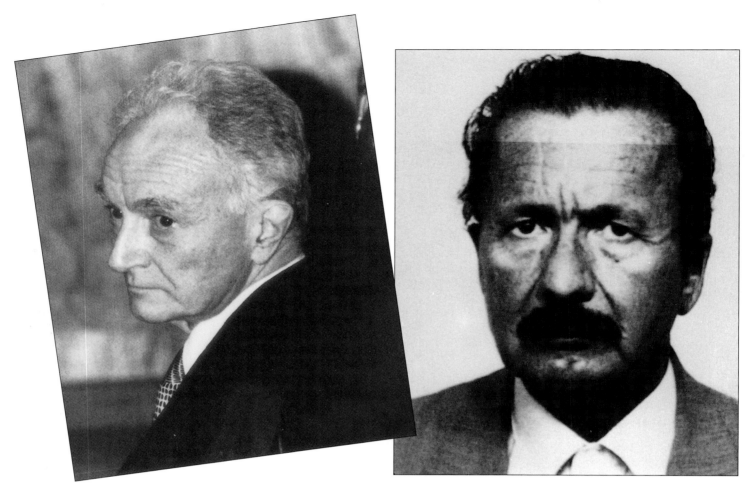

bribery and corruption, and virtually a right-wing shadow government. It was thus an ideal source of business for Calvi, who traded an ability to move money around the globe in return for favours and protection.

When Sindona's empire collapsed under the weight of the 1973 oil crisis, his protegé in Milan took on much of his work, and the next few years saw him master of the largest private bank in Italy which had achieved remarkable growth over a number of years. Much of this growth was illusory. Shares were transferred between Calvi's companies at bewildering speed, each time at a higher price which was reflected in the assets recorded on the balance sheet. For example some shares given a book value of $200 each were only worth $66 on the open market. In the process, billions of lire were illegally leaving Italy for accounts in countries such as Switzerland, Peru and Argentina. Amazingly, only one employee knew what was going on.

Another layer of secrecy surrounded the people on whose behalf some of these deals were struck. It later emerged that massive sums were being moved around for the Istituto per le Opere di Religione (IOR), otherwise known as the Vatican bank. This was run by an American archbishop, Paul Marcinkus, who also organized the Pope's popular tours abroad. The IOR controlled eight of Ambrosiano's foreign subsidiaries, although no one could have known this at the time. The Vatican found it convenient to conceal its activities partly because it would have been politically embarrassing for a Catholic bank to have holdings in, say, Communist-controlled companies, and also because it allowed them secretly to support favoured causes such as the banned Polish trade union Solidarity. It has been suggested that the resolve of the new Pope John Paul I to clean up the Vatican's financial dealings was behind his mysterious death in September 1978. This was one

of a number of deaths of people who seemed about to damage Calvi's operation. The other deaths were less mysterious, involving Mafia-style point blank shootings.

Early in the 1980s, it all began to go horribly wrong. The Bank of Italy quickened its snail's-pace investigation into Banco Ambrosiano which had been prompted by many rumours and allegations, some made by the now-jailed Sindona. In 1981 two magistrates looking into Sindona's Mafia ties chanced upon a list of P2 members, and found Calvi's name alongside some of the most influential men in Italy. The resultant scandal brought down yet another Italian government, and led to Calvi's arrest on 20 May 1981.

He was sentenced to four years and a fine of 16 billion lire ($12 million) for illegal exports of currency. But the story did not end there. On appeal, he was released and returned to running his bank, attempting to retrieve his position with increasing desperation as the authorities closed in. He alone knew that Banco Ambrosiano had a $1 billion-plus shortfall in its accounts, made up of loans to its front organizations abroad. When the Bank of Italy wrote demanding that Calvi inform his fellow directors of the true position, he lost the support of his board for the first time. On Friday, 11 June he fled Italy using a forged passport. After driving across Europe, he checked into an insalubrious Chelsea hotel on the Tuesday, accompanied by one of his newer acquaintances, a Sardinian property contractor called Flavio Carboni.

Clearly afraid for his life, he hid in his room and made a series of frantic calls to associates and his family. It was not enough. During a period when his companions somewhat conveniently were nowhere to be found, he disappeared and was found strangled hanging from Blackfriars Bridge. His death was initially thought to be suicide, but the unlikeliness of an unfit 62-year-old

SPEAKING IN CODE

On the day Calvi died, his secretary, Graziella Corrocher, killed herself by jumping from the fourth floor of the Banco Ambrosiano building. She had been devoted to Calvi and like the rest of the staff was appalled at the revelations of his fraud. She left a note hoping that Calvi "be cursed a thousand times for the harm he has done to everyone at the bank, and to the image of the group we were once so proud of". She clearly knew little of Calvi's secret machinations, but this is not surprising. Calvi often said "When two people know a secret, it's not a secret any more," and talked in a strange code when facing difficult questions. "It's all right, the black cassocks are behind us" was his way of implying Vatican backing for some deal. Somehow the combination number he chose for his overnight case lock is fitting for a man who conjured money out of nothing: it would reveal its secrets if the dials were turned to 0-0-0-0.

clambering across scaffolding, weighed down with bricks, to hang himself from a girder, when he had enough barbiturates to kill him in his own room led to an open verdict. It is more likely he was drugged, carried by boat to the bridge at high tide, and then hanged. So many people wanted him dead, either in revenge or to protect their own crimes, that the British police hardly knew where to begin their enquiries – and their Italian counterparts were apparently not particularly cooperative.

Banco Ambrosiano finally collapsed in August 1982, by which time its 4,200 employees had discovered that their miraculously successful firm had a massive deficit on its books and no prospect of even modest success as just another Italian bank. The Vatican was eventually persuaded that it had some moral involvement in the affair, and paid $250 million to cover some of Ambrosiano's $1,287 million debts. The balance remains a mystery.

SCANDAL ON WALL STREET

It has been called Wall Street's Watergate: the fall of the US financial world's greatest insider dealer, closely followed by the dethroning of the king of the junk-bond dealers. The scandal of Boesky and Milken had repercussions for the whole of Wall Street, and marked the close of an era when the profits justified the means.

LEFT

Ivan Boesky leaves a federal court in New York after pleading guilty to fraud charges. He avoided a longer sentence by plea-bargaining.

During the 1980s, America's financial centre, Wall Street, saw the most frenzied burst of activity in its history. A new generation of dealers began to make its mark. Young, tough and ambitious, they found new sources of money and used these funds to attack blue-chip businesses. Corporations such as Revlon (bought in 1985 for $3 billion) were acquired by smaller companies in deals that turned the market on its head. Often such firms were then sold off in pieces to finance the original debt. The brash newcomers were known to cut a few corners, but the Reagan adminis-tration adopted a *laissez-faire* attitude to the financial markets.

Some of the new breed were known as arbitrageurs, who speculated by buying stock in companies which were known to be take-over targets. During take-over battles, these shares become highly volatile, and some shareholders were happy to sell and avoid any additional risk. Ivan Boesky, son of a Russian immigrant who ran a chain of Detroit delicatessens, was a successful arbitrageur in the 1970s. But as others joined this lucrative practice, profits shrank. From about 1982 he used his wide range of contacts to discover likely

ABOVE

In the hectic trading atmosphere of the New York Mercantile Exchange, Boesky's information gave dealers the chance to clean up.

Junk bond king Michael
Milken brought in the
public relations experts
to combat stories of his
insider trading. He
emerged with his
reputation in tatters,
but rich enough for it
not to matter.

take-over victims before the infor-mation was publicly available, and to trade in the target shares. His sources for this insider dealing were often the raiders themselves, who relished the extra pressure an arbitrageur share-holding put on a company.

Boesky became Wall Street's most feared arbitrageur, and, at $1,700 an hour, its best paid. If he was buying shares in your company, you were in trouble. He was a workaholic, arriving at his office at 6am every morning. There were 160 telephone lines to the suite occupied by Ivan F Boesky Inc, and three phones in his car.

On 14 November 1986 a shocked financial world learned that 49-year-old Boesky was a crook. He had agreed to pay the regulatory body the Securi-ties Exchange Commission (SEC) $100 million, half as a fine for insider trad-ing and the rest in illicit profit repay-ments. In the previous year, the SEC had imposed total fines of only $3.7 million for insider dealing, so this penalty exposed a whole new league of wrongdoing. As details of the story emerged, looks of surprise became worried expressions, for Boesky had been cooperating with the SEC by giv-ing information on his many contacts, and had even been wired during the last few months which gave the SEC first-hand evidence.

Boesky was tipped off to the police by investment banker Dennis Levine, who had pleaded guilty to using non-public information in a series of deals which netted him $12 million. Levine had an agreement giving him 5 per cent of the profits on shares he tipped, and 1 per cent for extra information on those Boesky held. The tips were top quality. For example, Boesky had bought 377,000 Nabisco shares in the week before its merger with Reynolds was announced, netting $4 million. A similar tip on the merger of InterNorth and Houston Natural Gas allowed him to make $4.1 million.

Boesky started to give names in return for the dropping of many charges against him. His revelations were particularly damaging to one of the major brokers, Drexel Burnham Lambert, and its junk-bond department-head Michael Milken. Junk bonds are high-yield, high-risk, non-investment grade shares which were used to raise the money for the billion-dollar mergers and leveraged buyouts financed by huge quantities of debt, which had made Milken the most powerful figure in the market for corporate control. These had boosted Drexel from obscurity to the fifth-largest brokerage in the country.

Boesky revealed that he and Milken had swapped confidential market information, and manipulated share prices. Drexel would also "park" shares with Boesky to avoid suspicion falling on it or its clients, guaranteeing any losses he might make. On one occasion Boesky was paid to buy MCA shares to keep the price up when a Drexel client was selling its stake in the corporation.

At the end of 1988, Drexel agreed to pay $650 million in penalties for its numerous offences, a massive sum which contributed towards it filing for bankruptcy in February 1990. Milken held out until 24 April that year. Having denied all the allegations against him, and run a public relations campaign that presented him as virtually a saint, he pleaded guilty to six counts of securities fraud. He paid a $600 million penalty – only $50 million more than his record earnings for 1987. Plea-bargaining led to the dropping of 92

A SHREWD DEALER

Throughout his career, Ivan Boesky has demonstrated a knack for the smart move.

● He financed his share dealing through a series of complex partnerships. In one 1980 arrangement, his investors received 45 per cent of profits, but paid for 95 per cent of losses.

● Having agreed the date on which the announcement of his fine and ban from the Stock Exchange, Boesky sold $1.32 billion worth of shares. It was called "the ultimate insider deal" – trading on advance information of his own demise. The SEC claims it allowed the sell-off to avoid a massive shedding later on which could have put the market into a downward spiral similar to the 1929 crash.

● He was allowed to pay his 1986 $50 million fine with shares in Cambrian and General Securities. A year later the SEC admitted they had dropped $13 million in value.

● He successfully argued that his repayment of illicit profits was tax-deductible.

● Boesky's massive 1986 shares sell-off meant he escaped the October 1987 stock market crash.

charges of racketeering and insider trading which could have doubled his eventual 10-year jail sentence (parole expected after three yers). Milken remains one of the world's richest men, worth about $1 billion.

Boesky's cooperation with the authorities earned him a lenient sentence and he was released from jail on 4 April 1990. His information led to the biggest government crackdown on Wall Street in American history. He has testified at several trials of associates accused of insider dealing. His estimated worth is $100 million.

THE CHEATING PREACHER

Jim Bakker was king of the TV evangelists, but behind his pious words were corruption and greed. When he finally fell, he left a gaping hole revealing fierce rivalries among the men of God.

In the 1980s there was a boom in tele-evangelism on the American networks. The airwaves were bursting with God-fearing preachers passing the words of the Lord to watching millions, imploring them to send money to further the Christian cause. It was slick, powerful, and it raised a lot of money. At the top of the pile was Jim Bakker, who performed a syrupy double-act with his wife Tammy Faye. He had an effective, emotional style: when hot tears flowed down his cheeks during a sermon, the viewers sent in $105,000. Bakker headed an organization called PTL. The letters stand for Praise the Lord, or People that love, and they also spelt money: PTL had an income of $129 million in 1986. The organization ran a church, a 2,300-acre religious theme park, a 504-room hotel and a shopping mall called Heritage USA near Charlotte close to the border between North and South Carolina. Dubbed the "Christian Disneyland", it drew 6 million visitors in 1986. PTL also had its own TV station whose output was networked on 1,200 channels, and the flagship programme was a fund-raising talk-show called the Jim and Tammy Bakker Show.

On 19 March 1987, at the peak of his success, Jim Bakker shocked the evangelical world by resigning. He claimed he was being blackmailed as part of a "diabolical plot" to gain control of PTL, and that he had been "wickedly

manipulated for treacherous former friends". In this claim he was referring in particular to his one-time decorator, and now rival preacher, Jimmy Swaggart. Swaggart was said to be trying to take over PTL, but was not involved in the blackmail. This focused on an admitted sexual encounter between Bakker and church secretary Jessica Hahn at Clearwater Beach Hotel, Florida, in 1980. It finally emerged that PTL made available to Ms Hahn a $265,000 account, allegedly as hush money. She later sold her story, and semi-nude pictures of herself, to *Playboy* magazine for a reported $1 million.

While he fought to clear his name, Bakker called in fellow minister Jerry Falwell as his caretaker to run PTL.

Falwell soon realized the organization was a can of worms, with large sums disappearing into the Bakkers' accounts for personal use, and allegations of homosexuality and wife-swapping. When he sent an aide to the beleaguered Bakkers asking if they needed help, he received an astonishing list of demands. Bakker wanted a $300,000 salary for himself, and one of $100,000 for his wife, plus of attorney's fees, hospital insurance, rights to books and records, a lakeside home in South Carolina, security guards, and a maid for a year. "I don't see any repentance there. I see greed, the self-centredness, the avarice that brought them down," said Falwell. On 6 May Bakker and his attorney the Reverend Richard Dortch were defrocked.

ABOVE

A weeping Bakker is escorted to a car to be taken to a State Correctional Institution for psychiatric evaluation.

While this "Holy War" went on, the Internal Revenue Service (IRS) began to take an interest in the vast tax-free sums PTL had accumulated. They discovered that the God-fearing Bakkers had pocketed $4.8 million from PTL between January 1984 and March 1987, including $1.6 million in salaries and bonuses in 1986. It also emerged that the Bakkers enjoyed a luxurious lifestyle, indulged in their enthusiasm for expensive hand-made cars, and even had air-conditioned kennels installed for their dogs. The IRS concluded that Bakker and his aides had profited excessively from donations to the ministry, and revoked PTL's tax-exempt status.

As a result of the investigation, Bakker and Dortch were indicted for fraud on 5 December 1988. The charges related to the sale of vacation holdings which had netted $158 million, of which at least $4 million had been diverted for personal use. By this time Falwell and the rest of the PTL board had resigned, claiming a bid for the discredited organization by Bakker had ruined their fund-raising efforts. PTL had filed for a bankruptcy reorganization, and a federal court had ordered the Bakkers and an associate to repay $7.5 million in wasted profits and mismanaged funds.

The following August, Richard Dortch pleaded guilty to fraud and conspiracy and was sentenced to 8 years and a $200,000 fine, having agreed to testify at the Bakker trial. This began shortly afterwards, but was delayed on the fourth day when Bakker was found cowering in his lawyer's office, convinced that the courtroom was inhabited by hostile animals. When the trial resumed, he did not deny the facts of his fraud or the diversion of $3.7 million to his own wallet, but claimed no criminal intent. His defence attorney, Harold Bender, said Bakker was "a man of love, compassion and character who cares for his fellow man". But he conceded "maybe somewhere along the line it did get off track". Things were so far off track

that Bakker was convicted on all 24 counts and sentenced to 45 years with a fine of $500,000.

This was a scandal not just because of the obvious large-scale wrongdoing, but because of the hypocrisy of the men of God, who attempted to justify their actions using Biblical language but were revealed to have practised decidedly un-Christian behaviour. Bakker was not the only tele-evangelist to fall from grace. In 1988 Jim Swaggart tearfully confessed to an unspecified "sin", later alleged to involve hiring prostitutes for pornographic acts. In October 1991 he was found driving erratically in a car shared with a prostitute and a pile of pornographic magazines. By this time the TV preachers and their Christian organization were so discredited that Jerry Falwell had disbanded Moral Majority, the religious and political organization he had set up 10 years previously in 1979, and went back on the road to preach. Meanwhile, Jim Bakker contemplates his sins in Minnesota federal prison.

MANNA FROM ABOVE

The fraud charges against Bakker and Dortch related to the sale of $1000 partnerships guaranteeing three days a year free lodging at Heritage USA for life. So many were sold that the accommodation commitments could not possibly be met. When warned of this by an aide, Bakker typically chose a Biblical reference in his reply, telling him not to worry as "there was always room at the inn". Actually the inn was overflowing: in 1986, between 1300 and 1700 people were being turned away from their promised lodgings every month. In 1990, 145,000 major contributors to PTL filed a damages lawsuit, and Bakker was found liable to the tune of $130 million. As the Lord giveth, so he taketh away . . .

INDEX

ACKNOWLEDGEMENTS

t=top b=bottom l=left r=right c=centre

British Film Institute: p67; The British Museum: p11; The Hulton-Deutsch Collection: pp10, 12, 14, 15, 19b, 20, 22, 23, 26, 28, 30t, 31, 32, 33t, 34, 38, 40, 43l and r, 44, 46, 47b, 48t and b, 50, 51, 56, 58, 59, 61t, 65b, 68; Jean-Loup Charmet: pp16, 17, 18, 33b, 35t and b; John Frost Historical Newspaper Service: pp25t and b, 30b, 34, 45, 47t, 49, 57, 60, 61b, 65t, 69, 70l and r, 71, 72, 73, 74, 76, 78; The Mansell Collection: pp13, 19t; Wide World Photos: pp24, 27, 29, 36, 37, 39, 41, 42, 52, 53, 54, 55, 57, 62, 63, 64l and r, 66, 69.